T0184789

Optimal Spending on Cybersecurity Measures

Optimal Spending on Cybersecurity Measures: DevOps aims to discuss the integration of risk management methodologies within the DevOps process.

This book introduces the cyber risk investment model, and the cybersecurity risk management framework within the DevOps process. This can be used by various stakeholders who are involved in the implementation of cybersecurity measures to safeguard sensitive data. This framework facilitates an organization's risk management decision-making process to demonstrate the mechanisms in place to fund cybersecurity measures within DevOps practices, and demonstrates the application of the process using a case study: Cascade. This book also discusses the elements used within DevOps, DevSecOps, and will define a strategic approach to minimize cybersecurity risks within DevOps known as DevRiskOps.

Features:

- Aims to strengthen the reader's understanding of industry governance, risk and compliance practices.
- Incorporates an innovative approach to assess cyber security initiatives with DevOps.
- Explores the strategic decisions made by organizations when implementing cybersecurity measures and leverages an integrated approach to include risk management elements into DevOps.

Optimal Spending on Cybersecurity Measures
DevOps

Tara Kissoon

CRC Press
Taylor & Francis Group
Boca Raton London New York

CRC Press is an imprint of the
Taylor & Francis Group, an **informa** business

First edition published 2024
by CRC Press
2385 NW Executive Center Drive, Suite 320, Boca Raton FL 33431

and by CRC Press
4 Park Square, Milton Park, Abingdon, Oxon, OX14 4RN

CRC Press is an imprint of Taylor & Francis Group, LLC

© 2024 Tara Kissoon

Reasonable efforts have been made to publish reliable data and information, but the author and publisher cannot assume responsibility for the validity of all materials or the consequences of their use. The authors and publishers have attempted to trace the copyright holders of all material reproduced in this publication and apologize to copyright holders if permission to publish in this form has not been obtained. If any copyright material has not been acknowledged please write and let us know so we may rectify in any future reprint.

Except as permitted under U.S. Copyright Law, no part of this book may be reprinted, reproduced, transmitted, or utilized in any form by any electronic, mechanical, or other means, now known or hereafter invented, including photocopying, microfilming, and recording, or in any information storage or retrieval system, without written permission from the publishers.

For permission to photocopy or use material electronically from this work, access www.copyright.com or contact the Copyright Clearance Center, Inc. (CCC), 222 Rosewood Drive, Danvers, MA 01923, 978–750–8400. For works that are not available on CCC please contact mpkbookspermissions@tandf.co.uk

Trademark notice: Product or corporate names may be trademarks or registered trademarks and are used only for identification and explanation without intent to infringe.

ISBN: 978-1-032-51894-7 (hbk)
ISBN: 978-1-032-51897-8 (pbk)
ISBN: 978-1-003-40435-4 (ebk)

DOI: 10.1201/9781003404354

Typeset in Adobe Caslon Pro
by Apex CoVantage, LLC

Contents

About the Author

 **Tara Kissoon** is multi-certified I.T. Risk & Security Leader with twenty-five years of technology experience, twenty years of experience in the financial services industry. Tara's educational background encompasses a Master of Science (MSc) in Information Security with Upper Class Honours at the University of London, Royal Holloway College, a Master of Business Administration (MBA) with Distinction at the University of Toronto, Rotman School of Management, a Certified Information Systems Auditor (CISA), a Certified Information Systems Security Professional (CISSP) and is licenced within the Life Licenced Qualification Program (LLQP). Details are located @ www.thevirtualmall.ca and www.it-rs.org.

Preface

The aim of this book is to discuss the integration of risk management methodologies with DevOps through the use of a cybersecurity risk management framework. Most conceptual models consider the dynamic environment, which is adaptable to changes that occur within the decision-making process. These models and frameworks rely on either specific scenarios or controlled conditions. As a result of the dynamic environment within the cybersecurity industry, mitigation strategies evolve to address emerging industry threats. These variations influence the conditions that were used within previous frameworks and economic models. Decisions regarding cybersecurity spending within organizations vary based on the stakeholders, specifically the funding available in comparison to the recommended security measures necessary for compliance. These executive decisions may be coloured with bias regarding the appropriate security baseline required to protect relevant information assets within the organization. The trade-off between the costs of implementing a security measure and the benefit derived from the implementation is not easily measured. Therefore, the lack of this information may impact the business leader's decision to fund security measures and the choice to further invest in developing new technology to drive innovation, business growth and customer satisfaction.

This book focuses on the integration of risk management methodologies when implementing cybersecurity measures within DevOps Programs. This book will integrate a cybersecurity risk management framework within the secure software development lifecycle (SSDLC), and demonstrate the application of the process using a case study. This book will discuss the elements used within DevOps and DevSecOps, and will define a strategic approach to minimize cybersecurity risks within DevOps known as DevRiskOps.

This book makes an industry contribution by assisting business leaders with choosing an appropriate risk mitigation strategy when implementing cybersecurity measures. The application of this framework within organizations will assist stakeholders with decisions pertaining to cybersecurity spending. In leveraging the review of additional studies, this book aims to utilize a case study methodology to demonstrate that risk-based decisions are necessary when implementing cybersecurity measures.

The case study methodology provides an in-depth view of a risk-taking organization's risk mitigation strategy within the bounds of an educational environment focusing on the following five areas identified within a digital cyber risk model: 1) technology landscape, 2) data classification, 3) risk management practices, 4) cost-benefit analysis for cybersecurity measures and 5) business objectives.

1

INTRODUCTION

This book shares a strategic framework that could be used by the various stakeholders involved in the implementation of cybersecurity measures within DevOps to safeguard sensitive data and leverages a data centric focus on the evolution of cyber-attacks. Through use of existing literature, it is apparent that a wide range of principles are relevant within the cybersecurity decision-making process. Specific security measures are important and should be implemented appropriately to alleviate cybersecurity threats within the DevOps life cycle. The information provided in this book will give the necessary data to show that the cybersecurity decision-making process is clearly integrated with DevOps and the economics of information security to include current risk management models.

Economic optimization of information security is an area of interest to researchers and executives in most organizations. From a financial viewpoint, cost-benefit analysis is necessary and impactful to justify cybersecurity spend as it relates to security measures within the DevOps life cycle. Previous authors have focused on either traditional practices or the organizational decision-making process of information security investments using cost-benefit analysis.

This book aims to discuss the integration of organizational decision making within cybersecurity spend to effectively articulate the business impact of cybersecurity risks within the DevOps life cycle. This book focuses on the integration of risk management practices with economics to support a balanced approach to implementing security controls within the DevOps life cycle. Each area was reviewed in-depth to provide an understanding of its application to cybersecurity and the decision-making process used when evaluating and investing in various security measures. Three global industry areas were analysed to gain a further understanding of current gaps as noted below.

1.1 Why are Current Implementations of Cybersecurity Frameworks Effective in Identifying, Monitoring and Responding to Cybersecurity Threats?

In analysing industry data, it is apparent that organizations currently leverage government and industry frameworks when implementing cybersecurity measures. The foundation of the decisions made by most stakeholders are based on ensuring compliance with government regulations, industry standards and internal policy.

In addition, most organizations have anonymously expressed that they have experienced a type of cybersecurity breach, prioritized as follows: 1) malware/ransomware, 2) phishing, 3) lost/stolen computer media and 4) external/data breach, where ninety-four percent of respondents expressed an average dollar loss of between $0-$1 million. Organizational stakeholders believe they can detect, respond to and monitor a security incident, however, they are not able to continuously prevent security incidents from occurring within their environment.

These stakeholders believe that their organization is in compliance with government and industry standards. An organization measures the effectiveness of the implemented cybersecurity framework according to the following priorities: 1) compliance, 2) audit/assurance testing, 3) key performance indicators, 4) capacity maturity models and 5) cost, considering the organization's risk profile.

What factors are used by an organization when investing in cybersecurity controls?

The decision-making mechanisms utilized by organizations when evaluating and implementing different security measures primarily focus on 1) compliance with government and industry regulations, 2) investment cost, 3) the impact of either a breach or fine, 4) either reputational or brand risk, and 5) ease of use by the business.

1.2 What Decision-Making Mechanisms are Organizations using when Evaluating Different Security Measures Prior to Implementation?

Stakeholders that make decisions on cybersecurity measures within their organizations include the following: 1) Chief Technology Officer (CTO), 2) Chief Information Security Officer (CISO), 3) Head of Business Line, 3) Chief Information Officer (CIO), and 5) Board of Directors. The CTO and CISO are the stakeholders primarily responsible for advising and funding the investments within their organization, and their organization's investment budget is between $1-$5 million dollars annually. Stakeholders are involved during the implementation of cybersecurity measures in the following ways: 1) directly involved in the decision-making mechanism, 2) attend meetings on evaluating cybersecurity measures, 3) involved in implementation activities related to cybersecurity measures, and 4) supporting the cybersecurity function.

It is apparent that organizations have actively implemented cybersecurity frameworks, yet there is a need to enhance the decision-making process to reduce the number and types of breaches, along with strengthening the implemented cybersecurity framework to facilitate a stronger preventative approach. In addition, the factors that are used by an organization when investing in cybersecurity controls are heavily focused on compliance with government and industry regulations. Lastly, the decision-making process utilized when evaluating, implementing and investing in cybersecurity controls is weighted towards the technology organization and, therefore, may be biased based on competing priorities.

Most organizations are faced with an array of choices when deciding on funding, as it relates to cybersecurity measures. Funding the investment cost to provide a secure environment can be complex.

Cost-benefit analyses, risk appetite and business trade-offs are some of the areas that are factored into the overall decision-making process. Most stakeholders indicate that the following areas are critical in an organization's decision-making process when allocating funds for cybersecurity measures:

Allocation of budget—Although stakeholders believe that their organization has allocated a large enough budget to respond to or detect a cybersecurity breach, it is apparent that their organization's cybersecurity budget is insufficient to ensure appropriate cybersecurity measures to prevent such breaches.

Ability to prevent a cybersecurity breach—Although stakeholders believe that their organization can detect a cybersecurity breach in a timely manner, it is apparent that their organization is unable to prevent a cybersecurity breach, as some stakeholders indicate that their organization has encountered more than 15 breaches.

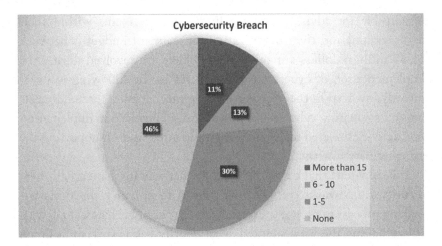

1.2.1 Measuring the Effectiveness of Implemented Frameworks

Stakeholders believe that their organization's current information security framework implementation is ineffective in preventing cybersecurity breaches. In addition, it is apparent that most organizations measure the effectiveness of their current information security framework implementation by 1) compliance with policy, 2) audit and assurance testing, 3) key performance indicators, 4) cost and 5) capacity maturity model.

1.2.2 Risk Level

Stakeholders indicate that their organization's decision-making process is aligned with a risk methodology, and as noted within most of the industry-recognized economic models, this methodology directly impacts the cost-benefit analysis.

1.2.3 Importance of Decision-Makers

It is apparent in most organizations that the decisions made by the CIO and head of the business line have similar priorities regarding 1) funding the investment cost, 2) implementing information security measures, and 3) reviewing the risk appetite statement. This parallel decision-making process may potentially have an adverse impact

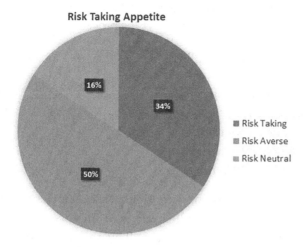

Risk Taking Appetite

on the decision to fund cybersecurity measures, especially in circumstances where the viewpoints are vastly different.

This book will examine risk management practices and applicable frameworks to define an appropriate cyber risk investment model for the implementation of information security measures within the DevOps life cycle.

1.3 DevOps

In general, the term DevOps is a combination of different phases within the traditional method, specifically it combines elements of the processes noted within the development and operations phases. DevOps involves performing several activities of application development in a specific order and is a wide term used for a combination of software development and IT operations. The DevOps approach consists of agility, continuous innovation, with scalability to build, test, consume, and develop software products. It champions an environment of experimentation, feedback, and constant learning to reinvent products.

The DevOps lifecycle is a compilation of automated processes and workflows that that occur within an iterative, continuous development lifecycle which is represented through an infinity loop resulting in faster delivery. Continuous development is a software development process that integrates multiple DevOps processes to include:

- Collaborative Development
- Continuous Integration
- Continuous Testing
- Continuous Feedback
- Continuous Monitoring
- Continuous Deployment
- Continuous Operations

The benefits of implementing continuous development processes in the application development lifecycle is to improve software quality with an automated DevOps process allowing organization to update and add new feature to products. This iterative approach allows organizations to identify errors, inefficiencies and vulnerabilities early in development. Therefore, increasing depth, breadth and repeatability in the testing cycle. Secondly, this type of process facilitates ease in resolving software errors, vulnerabilities and code defects while reducing project risk. By making incremental software updates, developers can identify whether the changes are effective. Finally with continuous feedback, productivity is improved as developers can accelerate software development by 1) eliminating code incompatibilities and conflicts, 2) providing immediate feedback, 3) Identifying code defects, errors and vulnerabilities, 4) enforcing quality gates through the project management office to ensure each software change is integrated, tested, and verified, and the release is a safe, secure, reliable, and high-quality product.

Continuous development is fully integrated within the DevOps lifecycle, and it is important to note that this lifecycle still requires planning and software development within a structured, continuous approach. The planning phase requires a clear understanding of the project's vision to include defining the source code requirements for a DevOps application. Following the development workflow, the continuous integration process automatically starts with several activities such as: 1) planning test cases for the following phase, 2) understanding the changes required within the software development phase to produce the desired outcome specified in the project requirements. The continuous integration of code into existing source code facilitates a reiterated development process which seamlessly integrates within the next phase of the DevOps lifecycle, continuous testing. This testing process examines the features within the application to include end-to-end testing resulting in transition from development to live environments through beta testing. The information derived from these testing scenarios and use cases are used to provide input into changes required within the continuous feedback process.

In the continuous monitoring phase, monitoring is designed into the software application's operational capabilities. When in a continuous use position, it may generate data about the application or appear in the form of files. This phase fixes errors within the system, for example unreachable servers, memory usage, and ensures the service's security and availability is appropriate. There are two critical phases within continuous feedback to make sure consistent improvements in the application code include continuous testing and continuous integration. Continuous feedback ensures these improvements are evaluated allowing developers to predict how these changes will affect the final product and includes use cases in which clients that tested these applications can share their experiences during this phase. The continuous deployment process includes regression testing which is used to ensure that any changes made to the code does not affect the operation of peripheral applications, for example high-traffic websites. New code is continuously deployed, and configuration management tools are crucial in executing tasks rapidly and frequently. Chef, Puppet, Ansible, and SaltStack are common tools used during this phase. Containerization tools are also critical during the deployment phase, such as Vagrant and Docker. These tools assist in driving consistency across the development, staging, testing, and production environments and aid in the soft scaling up and scaling down of instances. The final phase of the DevOps lifecycle, continuous operations is the simplest and most condense. The objective of continuous operation is to automate the release of the application and subsequent updates, resulting in this phase having shorter development cycles, allowing developers to continually accelerate the application's go-live date. In addition, all DevOps operations are founded on a continuous, automated, reiterated process, allowing the business unit to accelerate the final product with a quicker time-to-market release date.

In conclusion DevOps is primarily used to develop applications for e-commerce websites, cloud-native applications, and other large, distributed platforms. The integration of risk management practices within the DevOps Lifecycle will be discussed within this book.

2
DᴇᴠOᴘs

Continuous Deployment began with the emerging software development process successfully used and implemented by organization such as Facebook, Microsoft, and IBM. This process aims to facilitate immediate deployment of software to customers once new code is developed. This results in many organizational benefits to include: 1) business opportunities, 2) risk reduction for each release, and 3) creating of required software.

The aim of DevOps is to create efficiencies in the software delivery lifecycle which will enable continuous delivery to meet the on-going changes within organizations to include emerging trends and innovation. DevOps is implemented through a combination of people, processes and tooling to provide a continuous, automated, reiterative approach. Continuous Integration and Continuous Delivery are critical components in the DevOps lifecycle that enables the delivery of code faster and securely. The emphasis that DevOps places on collaboration through the change process assists organizations with the release of high-quality software in a quicker delivery method. DevOps encourages a culture of open-mindedness, predictability, cross-skill training and performing shared tasks to achieve an acceptable result in developing and deploying applications, for example web applications.

The overall goal of DevOps is to improve the business value of the work completed in technology and to focus on the following goals:

- Deliver measurable business value through continuous and high-quality service delivery.

DOI: 10.1201/9781003404354-2

- Emphasize simplicity and agility in all areas, including technology, process and human factors.
- Break down barriers between development and operations by enabling trust and shared ownership, supporting innovation and encouraging collaboration.
- Manage dynamic compliance, as access/sharing laws change rapidly.

Specifically,

1. Agile and lean refer to teams iterate, with short development cycles and fast feedback. Agile focuses on culture and is agnostic in relation to the tools used.
2. DevOps refers to how engineering organizations collaborate using cross-functional teams. DevOps starts with culture and drives towards tooling.
3. System reliability engineering (SRE) refers to how engineering organizations automate, entrusting highly scaled operations to people with a software engineering mindset. SRE starts with tooling and drives towards culture.
4. DevOps variants (such as "SecDevOps") involve the insertion or addition of another organization/practice early in the SDLC, and the prevalence of these different types of DevOps speaks to the increasing integration of functions in modern organizations.

2.1 Agile DevOps

Agile DevOps integrates the Agile process within operations into DevOps to facilitate faster feedback. In Agile, a review is completed at every sprint, and can be considered a subset of DevOps that focuses on the implementation of a collaborative development. Although DevOps is similarly built on the idea of getting fast feedback, it is important to note that a project may vary and therefore a project can be agile without employing DevOps practices whereas another project utilizes the waterfall methodology however still employs DevOps practices throughout the lifecycle.

"Disciplined Agile® Delivery (DAD) is a people-first, learning-oriented hybrid agile approach to IT solution delivery. DAD addresses all aspects of the full delivery life cycle, supporting multiple ways of working that can be tailored for the project context. DAD encompasses all aspects of agile software development in a robust, pragmatic, and governable manner." Project Management Institute, pmi.org.

DevOps facilitates the incorporation of many variations, however elements from the following capabilities are common to most DevOps cultures: 1) collaboration, 2) automation, 3) continuous planning, 4) collaborative development, 5) continuous integration, 6) continuous delivery, 7) continuous testing, 8) continuous operations, 9) continuous monitoring and 10) continuous learning.

2.2 Collaboration

Development and IT operations work together, and DevOps extends far beyond the technology organization due to the need for collaboration, which extends to all stakeholders in the delivery of software.

"The foundation of DevOps success is how well teams and individuals collaborate across the enterprise to get things done more rapidly, efficiently and effectively".—Tony Bradley, Scaling Collaboration in DevOps, DevOps.com.

Collaboration in many organizations may be difficult to achieve since certain functions are siloed. One of the challenges within the Devops process is achieving organizational-wide culture and cross-team collaboration. Organizations employ various strategies to address these challenges and create effective collaboration between cross-functional teams to include: 1) using collaboration technology and automation, 2) creating a roadmap and refining the project plans, 3) creating an effective communication plan, 4) building a hybrid work policy, 5) creating an inclusive hybrid environment, 5) having a transparent process to identify and resolve challenges, and 6) encouraging diverse ideas.

2.3 Automation and Tools

DevOps relies heavily on automation and tools, and uses toolchains to automate large parts of the end-to-end software development and deployment process.

DevOps tools play a critical role in solving the problem of integration between environments. These tools once implemented blend various systems together and work continuously enabling source code changes to propagate across different environments. Today, organizations are challenged with finding the appropriate tool, therefore selection of appropriate DevOps tooling is important within the automation and integration of different systems.

In general, Open-Source tools are used by many software delivery programs to enable automation within various phases of the DevOps lifecycle. This allows organizations to leverage internal frameworks which determines the maturity level of the DevOps project implementation.

There are several tools that are used within DevOps, a few examples are:

- Jira is a tool that is used to sprint plan, create stories and issues, track the issues with labelled priority and release software.
- Confluence is a knowledge base tool used to create, collaborate and provide a common repository for documents.
- Gitlab is the first application built in support of the DevOps lifecycle. This tool provides a way for teams to collaborate through a single conversation across various platforms.
- Docker is a tool that allows the application to be self-contained in an isolated environment.
- Jenkins is an open-source integration server which facilitates software development related to building, testing and deployment.
- Artifactory is a repository manager which organizes build artefacts and libraries centrally.
- SonarQube performs continuous automatic analysis of code against various code quality rules to detect bugs and code smells on programming languages.

2.4 Continuous Planning

Continuous planning connects business strategy and customer feedback into the development lifecycle to align investment options with the organization's cost benefit analysis. This uses lean principles to facilitate small teams through identification of outcomes and resource requirements to validate the business value. In addition, continuous planning requires a process to continually adapt and adjust as product backlog is maintained, divided into smaller releases based on priority while measuring actual progress and customer requirements to facilitate an agile shift within teams.

Continuous planning in DevOps assists team to plan, monitor and change their development process as needed. This enables flexibility within teams to adapt quickly to changes within business requirements, customer feedback and technology advances. This involves establishing goals and a clear understanding of the project to be able to move forward in an effective manner. Continuous planning also involves identifying risks and dependencies, to make sure that teams can proactively address any potential issues. Lastly, it requires regular communication with stakeholders and team members to keep the project on track.

Continuous planning is a critical element of DevOps, allowing teams to make effective decisions quickly, creating a roadmap for the development process, anticipating delays and adjusting plans based on changing requirements. This helps to ensure that the DevOps process is constant and consistent resulting in a high-quality product being delivered on time. Additionally, continuous planning assists organization with staying ahead of trends and customer needs giving the organization a competitive advantage.

There are several risks associated with omitting continuous planning in the DevOps lifecycle. These include: 1) an impact to product quality, 2) requirements being undefined, 3) unmet deadlines, 4) vague scope, 5) dysfunctional team, and 6) increased cost. Therefore implementing effective continuous planning entails: 1) a well-defined DevOps strategy, 2) establishing a Plan-Do-Check-Act Cycle, 3) developing, mapping, adapting, automating, improving and communicating a continuous planning process, 4) measuring and monitoring progress, 5) integrating adoption while managing compliance, 6) integrating continuous planning within the organizational culture and technology, 8) integrating continuous planning into the software delivery lifecycle, 9) integrating industry trends, and 9) refining continuous planning practices.

2.5 Collaborative Development

Collaborative Development is defined as a process for integrating, collaborating and providing an iterative approach within the DevOps lifecycle within technology, and is accountable for processes within areas such as: operations, application development, quality assurance and infrastructure development. Collaborative Development interconnects business, development and quality assurance to deliver a faster end result which includes innovation and customer experiences. This significantly changes the method that clients can utilize to build their applications and drive tangible business outcomes. The technological enablers for DevOps establish capabilities through automating tasks. In addition, automation provides a pipeline to production for a specific software environment with the ability to integrate across the entire DevOps environment.

Collaborative product development is a strategy, process and set of software applications that allow various organizations to work together on the development of a cross organizational product and can utilize phases within the collaborative development approach for software delivery.

2.6 Continuous Integration

Continuous integration is essential in the DevOps culture because DevOps emerged from an agile culture, and continuous integration is a fundamental tenet of the agile approach where developers merge their code changes in a central repository following the automated build and test process. Continuous integration most often refers to the build or integration stage of the software release process and entails both an automation component (i.e a CI or build service) and a cultural component (i.e. learning to integrate frequently). The goals of continuous integration are to resolve coding bugs quicker, improve software quality, and reduce the time it takes to validate and release new software updates. Continuous integration is required to address the pitfalls within the traditional development process. Specifically, developers worked siloed for an extended period and implemented their code once completed resulting in difficulties in merging code changes, code errors being unresolved and extending project and customer timelines.

Continuous integration allows developers to deposit their code changes to a common repository using version control mechanisms such as Git. Prior to each commit, developers have the option to initiative unit tests on their code as a verification prior to integrating. Therefore, a continuous service automatically builds and runs unit tests on the new code changes to immediately surface any errors.

2.7 Continuous Testing

Continuous testing is a software development process in which applications are tested repeatedly throughout the software development life cycle (SDLC). The testing cycle may include: 1) unit testing, 2) API testing, 3) integration testing, 4) system testing and 5) acceptance testing. The focus is to 1) evaluate software quality 2) provide early critical feedback, and 3) enable faster time to market with enhanced quality.

The continuous testing process within the DevOps lifecycle is critical. Continuous testing starts in the development environment where developers build quality into the code, provide test data sets and meet the challenge of quick turnaround not only by automating the test process but also by redefining test methodologies.

Continuous testing creates a central system of decision that helps assess application business risk. When applied consistently, it guides development teams to meet business expectations and visibility when making informed decisions in order to optimize the business value of a release.

Operations ensures that monitoring tools are in place and test environments are properly configured. They can participate in functional, load, stress and leak tests, and offer analysis based on their experience with similar applications running in production.

The test function in a DevOps environment helps developers balance quality and speed using automated tools to reduce the cost of testing and allows test engineers to leverage their time more effectively. Most importantly, continuous testing shortens test cycles by allowing integration testing earlier in the process.

Continuous testing also eliminates testing bottlenecks through virtualized, dependent services and simplifies the creation of virtualized test environments that can be easily deployed, shared and updated as systems change. These capabilities reduce the cost of provisioning and maintaining test environments and shorten test cycle times by allowing integration testing earlier in the lifecycle.

Continuous Testing employs an automated way to reduce effort and time required in delivering acceptable results. This eliminates bottleneck in the testing cycle by using virtualized dependent services to simplify the test environments. This method reduces the costs of provisioning and maintaining the various test environments.

2.8 Continuous Delivery

Amazon Web Services (AWS) defines continuous delivery as a DevOps "software development practice where code changes are automatically built, tested and prepared for a release to production". Continuous delivery expands upon continuous integration by deploying all code changes to a testing environment and/or a production environment after the build stage. When continuous delivery is implemented properly, developers will always have a deployment-ready build artefact that has passed through a standardized test process.

The actual release frequency can vary greatly depending on the company's legacy and goals. High-performing organizations using DevOps achieve multiple deployments per day compared to medium performers who release once per week to once per month.

Exactly what is released varies depends on the organization. In some organizations, QA and operations triage potential releases: 1) many interact directly with users, 2) some cycle back to development, and 3) a few simply are not deployed at all. In comparison, other organizations transition from developers to users, relying on real-time monitoring and rapid remediation to minimize the impact of a rare failure. It is important to note that because each update is small, the chance of failure is significantly reduced.

Continuous delivery enables businesses to reduce cycle time to obtain faster feedback from users, reduce the risk and cost of deployments, gain visibility of the delivery process and manage the risks of software delivery more effectively.

From a risk and compliance perspective, continuous delivery is a more mature, efficient and effective method of applying controls to meet regulatory requirements than the traditional combination of automated and manual activities.

2.9 Continuous Release & Deployment

Continuous deployment is a software development strategy where automatic code changes are released to the production environment. This is driven by a series of automated predefined tests, once new updates pass these tests, the system directly releases the updates.

Continuous deployment creates the ability to receive early feedback from relevant stakeholders which enables steady and stable releases. This improves the quality of the product, enables trust and strengthens customer satisfaction. It also enables teams to perform on demand self-deployments which continuously integrates software driven innovation.

2.10 Continuous Operations

Continuous operations occurs at the end of the DevOps pipeline and plays a critical role in the planning and design, as they are activities that are 24 hours / 7 days per week and sustained during business disruption. Continuous operations provide the structure to adequately manage an application and ensure that the application meets all applicable requirements (i.e. compliance, service levels). It influences continuous development to assure that the application source code can be managed after continuous delivery and ensures continuous compliance and runtime security intelligence. Continuous operations provide improved quality control, higher output and lower production costs.

2.11 Continuous Monitoring

Given the high number of releases in a continuous delivery environment, it is difficult to implement the rigorous pre-release testing typically required in waterfall development approaches. In a DevOps environment, failures must be found and fixed in real time. With continuous monitoring, teams measure the performance and availability of software to improve stability. Continuous monitoring helps identify the root causes of issues quickly to proactively prevent outages and minimize user issues. Some monitoring experts even advocate that the definition of a service must include monitoring, as it is viewed as integral to service delivery.

Similar to testing, monitoring starts in development. The same tools used to monitor the production environment can be employed in development to identify performance problems before a product moves into production. Two kinds of monitoring are required for DevOps: 1) server monitoring and 2) application performance monitoring.

Continuous Monitoring automates and optimizes the ability to monitor and manage the performance and availability of applications and infrastructure continuously. It provides a dashboard on performance which assists in identification of changes and remediation activities.

The main areas for monitoring in a DevOps implemented project Include: 1) Application Performance Management, 2) IT Operations Analytics, and 3) Operational Problem Management.

Effective logging actively monitors application logs and works at multiple levels to analyse the logs by providing details when needed. The logs are analysed to assist the development team in performing root cause analysis, sharing the end results derived from the log analysis, and providing quality feedback.

2.12 Continuous Learning—Continuous Customer Feedback and Optimization

Customer feedback integrated within this process provides for improved decision making and optimization. An early and rapid feedback from the systems assists on saving time and improving the end user experience on a continuous basis. The DevOps maturity model enables growth through continuous learning among development and operations teams. The capabilities and skills defined, guarantees enhanced ability to handle issues of scale and complexities. Information Technology Infrastructure Library, ITIL is a framework of best practices for IT service management which focuses on aligning IT services according to the needs of the business. The degree of DevOps implementation can also be measured by means of maturity models against various matrices. Each of these tools serving one of the DevOps phases are unique in its own ways and provide different features while making optimum use of the tools for the right purpose. These tools are used to design, build, deploy, test, monitor, manage and operate software and systems connected as one integrated pipeline. The cost of these services depends on the volume and usage across the platform.

3

SECURE DEVELOPMENT LIFECYCLE

3.1 DevSecOps

Transitioning to a DevOps architecture or the cloud, and rebuilding applications require significant changes in technological oversight and resources. Changes to the development teams and internal procedures are required to provide the agility needed within a DevOps environment. Specifically, activities such as: 1) team members, roles and responsibilities need to be redefined, and 2) adopting new tools. In addition, incorporating security requirements and risk management practices within the DevOps lifecycle is important to address potential security threats.

Development, Security, and Operations (DevSecOps) integrates security requirements into the DevOps process. DevSecOps is a secure software development process where secure measures are implemented within the development lifecycle to ensure application confidentiality, integrity and availability.

In addition, cybersecurity activities such as implementing a secure architecture, governance, identity and access management (IAM), secure code review, configuration, and vulnerability management are included within DevSecOps to enable the rapid application delivery and reducing the requirement for post-implementation resolutions.

DevSecOps involves introducing security within the phases of the software development life cycle (SDLC) which integrates the security teams within development and operations. DevSecOps is aligned with DevOps as it requires a shift in culture, process and tools across core functional teams making security a shared responsibility and building security into the DevOps continuous integration and continuous

DOI: 10.1201/9781003404354-3

delivery (CI/CD) workflow in both the pre-production and production environments.

DevSecOps integrates security testing in every phase of the software development lifecycle to include tools and processes which facilitates collaboration between team members to design, build and implement software in a secure and efficient manner. Ultimately, DevSecOps is significant as it ensures security requirements are seamlessly integrated within the software development and deployment lifecycle.

3.2 Secure System Development Lifecycle

A secure system development lifecycle (SDLC) process ensures that security assurance activities, such as penetration testing, code review and architecture analysis, are an integral part of the development effort. Activities within each phase assist in the mitigation of vulnerabilities and management of risk.

3.2.1 Planning

In the first phase of the systems development process, the need for a new system to achieve the business's strategic objectives is identified. This is a preliminary plan or a feasibility study for acquiring the resources to modify or improve a service. The purpose of this step is to determine the scope of the problem and identify solutions. The resources, costs, time and benefits should be considered at this stage.

The feasibility study should incorporate the following:

- Assessment of the impact on the existing environment.
- Staff development and resource requirements.
- Project development cost analysis.
- Program maintenance costs.
- Evaluation of alternative project implementation approaches, such as build versus buy and outsourcing.
- Description of the proposed solution.
- Risks associated with the proposed solution.
- Benefit analysis, including cost reduction, error reduction, new customers and improved customer service.

- Involvement of information security teams to ensure that appropriate security concerns have been incorporated into the feasibility study.

3.2.2 Requirements

This phase defines how an organization will focus on the source of its problem or the need for a change. In the event of a problem, possible solutions should be submitted and analysed to identify the most appropriate ways to address the goals of the project.

Business and operational requirements specifications should be developed to ensure that the project requirements that are necessary to support business objectives are understood. Users and development teams generally lead this process. The business requirements should consider the following issues:

- Data that are required to support the system or application and how it relates to other data.
- Frequency of use of the system or application.
- Required response time for online processing.
- Function relations to and dependencies on other components.
- Identification of applicable legal or regulatory requirements or constraints.
- Anticipated life span of the system or application.

Operational requirements should consider the following issues:

- Security requirements.
- Contingency requirements.
- Distributed and centralized processing requirements.
- Data input strategy and responsibility.
- Data retention requirements.
- Output distribution requirements.
- Expected transaction volumes, including project transaction growth.
- Critical system performance requirements.

Information security teams should be involved throughout the business and operational requirements phase to ensure that security concerns are properly addressed and reflected in the requirements document. The risk assessment methodology is performed mainly during this phase to provide early security perspectives for the project team.

3.2.3 Design

This phase involves describing the necessary specifications, features and operations that will satisfy the functional requirements of the proposed system. It includes the ability to transpose the business and operational requirements into functional requirements to reflect the anticipated user experience associated with the system or application. Functional specifications reflect the user's perspective, which has been translated into the preliminary design. For maintenance and enhancement activities, the focus is on using a before/after description to document what will change.

Functional specifications should include the following:

- Data flow diagrams: tracing data through all their processing points.
- Data definitions: defining data, data relationships and naming conventions.
- Screen definitions: defining input fields and checking ranges.
- Inputs: sources of inputs, types of data and description of data.
- Report definitions: describing reports, the data to be contained in each report, how the data values are derived and the users who utilize specific reports.
- Control and security requirements: inputting editing requirements, audit log trails for critical data from the point of origin to the point of disposition, and audit log trails for the use of privileges and identifying critical processing areas.
- System interface requirements: identifying interaction points between this system and other systems, anticipated inputs and outputs, response time expectations, and other intersystem dependencies.
- Backup, restart and recovery: determining the frequency of backup, rationale behind backup, backup retention requirements, restart requirements specifying how the application should be restarted and recovery requirements.

- Contingency requirements: conducting an analysis to determine how long the application can be unavailable before the business is affected and identifying datasets, software and other items that need to be restored at an offsite processing centre.
- Hardware requirements: determining communication requirements, disk space, and processing equipment.
- Service-level requirements: determining uptime requirements, required response times, critical windows, deadlines for input, and deadlines for report distribution.
- Capacity requirements: determining transaction volumes and expected growth.
- Conversion requirements: developing a method to be used to create data on the new system, a method to reconcile data during conversion, cutover requirements, and a process for verifying converted data.

During the functional specifications process, information security teams should generally be involved in supporting the project team's efforts to capture the preliminary design and functional description of the system or application. Functional specifications should include security-related information such as technical features, i.e., access controls and operational practices (i.e., awareness and training). Information security teams should review and provide feedback on this document prior to the detailed design phase.

3.2.4 Development

This phase entails engaging the programmer, network engineer and/or database developer in the project. The work includes using a flow chart to ensure that the process is organized. The development phase signifies the end of the initial section of the process and the start of code development. Specifically, code is produced according to the requirements produced in the design phase.

In the development phase, the system's or application's security features are developed, configured and enabled, and the program specifications are used to describe the program logic and processing requirements. The program specifications are developed as part of this phase prior to the commencement of programming. These specifications provide the requirements necessary to determine the steps needed to code the programs.

Information security teams should retain the right to perform source code reviews for critical aspects of the system or application, including user authentication, authorization and financial transactions. Source code reviews should have an enhanced focus on code provided by third parties, including offshore development organizations.

3.2.5 Testing

This phase involves system integration and system testing of programs and procedures, which is normally carried out by a quality assurance (QA) professional to determine whether the proposed design meets the initial set of business goals. Testing may be repeated, specifically to check for errors, bugs and interoperability, and should be performed until the end user finds the results acceptable. Another part of this phase is verification and validation, both of which will help ensure successful completion.

3.2.5.1 Unit Testing Unit testing is an integral part of the agile software development process which aims to identify and resolve bugs through a review of isolated sections of code. The unit test criteria should include the following:

- File updating, merging and sorting.
- All decision logic.
- All system or application interfaces, integration testing.
- Invalid transactions and the related error-handling routines.
- Restart/recovery routines.
- Stress testing.
- Error conditions.
- Page counters and overflow headers.

3.2.5.2 System Testing During the system testing phase, code development for the project is completed, and testing is performed to ensure that all functions work as required.

The system test environment is typically shared among all programmers with strictly controlled changes to the environment.

System test criteria should include the following:

- Verification that all functionality is performed as specified by the functional and design specifications.
- Program interfaces.
- Other system interfaces.
- Restart and recovery procedures.
- Transaction validation and rejection.
- Transaction processing cycles.
- System or application performance criteria.
- System or application output generation.
- Stress testing.
- Error handling.
- Input/output verification.
- Procedures and restrictions regarding the use of production data.
- Complete and accurate audit log trails.
- Security testing, i.e., authentication, authorization.
- System or application security testing, i.e., ethical hacking.
- Code reviews of critical sections of code and externally developed code.

Where possible, system or application security testing should be executed using an automated testing tool. This will support the creation of tests and procedures that can be used for regression testing during future enhancements.

3.2.5.3 Parallel Test Plan Where an existing system or application is in place, parallel testing ensures that the functions within a simulated production environment are equivalent to the existing process.

During the system testing phase, information security teams should be deeply involved in reviewing the security tests written by the project/test team and validating the security testing results. Security teams may also elect to perform a penetration test to ensure that the development team considers common security vulnerabilities.

3.2.5.4 Deployment Involves the actual installation of the newly developed system and/or application. This step puts the project into production by moving the data and components from the old system into the new system through a direct cutover. While this can be a complicated transition, the cutover typically occurs during off-peak hours, thus minimizing the risk.

The cutover/installation plan documents the transition from an old system or application to a new one. This plan should address any migration of production data that has not been performed. It should also address the installation activities and coordination with system users. Fallback procedures should be defined in the event of an erroneous transition.

3.2.5.5 Maintenance This phase involves maintenance and requires regular updates. During this step, end users can refine the system to boost performance, add new capabilities or meet additional user requirements. It also includes a post-implementation review, conformance and defect tracking.

3.2.6 Post-implementation Review

A post-implementation review ensures that the system or application is operating at a satisfactory level. This review involves soliciting user feedback on the overall effectiveness of the project and the achievement of the requirements and timelines. This information provides valuable insight for future projects and identifies potential shortcomings in the SDLC.

Security teams should participate in the post-implementation review to confirm that the security capabilities deployed are satisfactory.

At this time, the documentation of all security decisions made in support of the system or application is finalized, and variances from existing security policies and standards are noted. Where variances are permitted on a temporary basis, tracking is initiated to ensure that they are resolved in accordance with an agreed-upon schedule.

3.2.7 *Conformance and Defect Tracking*

The project management process should ensure conformance with all aspects of the SDLC. In this context, conformance refers to ensuring that the documents itemized above are created, reviewed and approved before the next phase of the SDLC.

Any modifications to a document, once approved, should be reviewed, and all impacted groups should agree on the change. Defect-checking tools should be used to monitor, and track identified defects during all testing phases. This provides a basis for making informed decisions regarding the status and resolution of any defects.

3.3 Secure Development Lifecycle

The secure software development lifecycle (SSDLC) is the process of including security artefacts in the SDLC process.

An SSDLC is a framework that defines the process used by organizations to build an application from its inception to decommission. Throughout the years, multiple standard SDLC models have been proposed (waterfall, iterative, agile) and integrated in multiple ways within various organizational environments.

3.3.1 *Planning and Requirements*

The first step in any initiative is to map out a planning process. During this phase, an organization must identify the release theme, contents and timeline. This phase typically includes activities such as collecting end-user requirements, determining user stories to include in the release, and planning release phases and dates.

Key considerations during this phase include the following:

- Ensuring that an application meets business requirements.
- Engaging in threat modelling/secure design
- Choosing the language and libraries to use in the development process.
- Mapping test cases to business and functional requirements

3.3.2 *Architecture and Design*

In the architecture and design phase, the organization's technology teams should follow the architecture and design guidelines to address identified risks. In addition, this phase evaluates the planned system design and potential integration with other systems, as well as the incorporation of shared services and common security controls, including the following:

- Authentication
- Disaster recovery
- Intrusion detection
- Incident reporting

When vulnerabilities are addressed early in the design phase, processes include threat modelling and architecture risk analysis to assist in simplifying and providing a secure development process.

3.3.3 *Test Planning*

Applying security controls in the testing phase should be considered carefully and planned logically. The intent is to integrate the controls into existing systems, therefore challenges to system performance should be discovered early. Additionally, some security controls may limit or hinder normal development activities.

For new information systems, the security requirements identified and described in the appropriate system security plans should be designed, developed and implemented.

The system security plans for operational information systems may require the development of additional security controls to supplement in-place controls or the modification of controls that are deemed less than effective.

During this phase, decisions are made based on integration challenges and trade-offs. It is important to document major decisions and business/technology drivers.

In cases where the application of a planned control is not possible or advisable, compensatory controls should be considered and documented.

3.3.4 Coding

During the development phase, the organization's development teams should train developers in secure coding practices. While performing the usual code review to ensure that the project has the specified features and functions, developers should minimize security vulnerabilities introduced in the code by integrating secure coding practices, i.e., OWASP. Specifically, the source code should be periodically reviewed using automated tools or manual spot checks for common programming errors that have a detrimental impact on system security, including the following:

- Cross-site scripting vulnerabilities.
- Buffer overflows.
- Race conditions.
- Object model violations.
- Poor user input validation and error handling.
- Exposed security parameters.
- Passwords in the clear.
- Violations of stated security policy, models, or architecture as part of the software development QA process.
- Using open-source components in a secure way.
- Static code analysis.
- Vulnerability scanning.

3.3.5 Testing and Results

To reduce redundant functional and security testing activities, the following recommendations are made:

- Functional test plans should include general security feature testing to the greatest extent possible.
- Preliminary testing of basic security controls should be performed during functional testing to reduce or eliminate issues earlier in the development cycle, i.e., mandatory access controls, secure code development, and firewalls.
- Preliminary testing is considered development-level testing, not certification and accreditation (C&A) testing, and if no

changes occur, test results should be reused to the greatest extent possible in the C&A.

- For systems of high visibility and sensitivity, independent development testing should be considered.
- Preliminary testing should be completed at the component or security zone level to ensure that each component or security zone is secure as an entity.
- The process and results of all security testing that occurs throughout the lifecycle should be captured for evaluation, issue identification, and potential reuse.

The following vulnerability assessments should also be considered during this phase:

- Dynamic code analysis
- Penetration testing
- Ethical hacking
- Password hacking

When implementing DevSecOps, organizations should consider a variety of application security testing (AST) tools to integrate within various stages of their continuous integration and continuous deployment processes, tools such as:

- Static application security testing (SAST).
- Software composition analysis (SCA).
- Interactive application security testing (IAST).
- Dynamic application security testing (DAST).

3.3.6 Release and Maintenance

After deployment and implementation, security practices should be followed throughout software maintenance. Applications should be regularly updated and assessed as follows:

- Security assessment
- Vulnerability scanning
- Penetration testing
- Ethical hacking

3.4 Cloud Environments

Vulnerability management is the process of identifying, classifying, remediating and mitigating vulnerabilities, especially in software and firmware. This process becomes complex in a cloud-based environment, as various layers of technology can be managed by different organizations based on the implementation. An organization's vulnerability management program should extend to ensuring that vendor-managed cloud-based solutions have appropriate controls in place to align with the organization's risk appetite and risk tolerance.

3.4.1 Vulnerability Scanning in a Cloud Environment

The differences between traditional technology environments and cloud-based environments arise primarily from 1) an organization outsourcing the ability to own and control the infrastructure for cloud services to an external vendor and 2) the organization being unable to access the vulnerability data of native cloud services. There is an inability to associate the data with cloud native vulnerabilities, as CVE IDs are not generally assigned to them. Therefore, it becomes difficult for the organization as a client to make an informed, risk-based decision regarding a vulnerable cloud service. For example, when should the organization decide to reject the risk and stop using a cloud service or accept the risk and continue using the service?

Furthermore, even if CVE IDs are assigned to cloud native vulnerabilities, the differences between traditional and cloud environments are so vast that vulnerability data that are normally associated with a CVE in a traditional environment are inadequate for cloud service vulnerabilities. For example, in a traditional IT environment, CVEs are linked to a software version, and the organization can determine whether a software is vulnerable by checking the version. In cloud services, the software version is usually known only to the cloud service provider. Therefore, the organization as a client may be unable to apply security controls or other mitigations to address the risk of a vulnerability.

Owing to these differences, the cloud provider should consider including vulnerability data that are useful in the context of a cloud service. Specifically, vulnerability data provided by the cloud provider would provide the organization with the ability to make risk-based decisions, including whether to continue or stop using a cloud service.

EXAMPLE: Vulnerability Scanning in Amazon Web Services Elastic Container Registry

The AWS Electric Container Registry (ECR) is a fully managed container registry that makes it easy for developers to store, manage and deploy container images. Image scanning is an automated vulnerability assessment feature in an ECR that helps improve the security of an organization's application container images by scanning them for a broad range of OS vulnerabilities.

3.4.2 Implement Image Scanning for Containers

Container security comprises a range of activities and tools involving developers, security operations engineers, and infrastructure administrators. One crucial link in the cloud native supply chain is scanning container images for vulnerabilities and to obtaining actionable insights. ECR image scanning uses the ECR native solution and provides an implementation strategy for a specific use case and scheduled re-scans as the foundation.

3.4.3 Prevent Images with Known Vulnerabilities from Entering Production

An organization can enable image scans or push for its repositories to ensure that every image is automatically checked against an aggregated set of CVEs. The AWS ECR uses the severity of a CVE from an upstream distribution source if available; otherwise, the common vulnerability scoring system (CVSS) score can be used to obtain the National Vulnerability Database vulnerability severity rating. This can assist an organization with automated detection and responses to container image vulnerabilities prior to promoting and deploying an image into production.

There are two kinds of scanning.

Static scanning is performed in environments prior to deployment with the implication that developers (or secops) can detect vulnerabilities before a container is launched. ECR image scanning falls under this category; that is, it enables an organization to scan OS packages in container images for CVEs, a public list of known security threats, without the need for an organization to set up its own scanning infrastructure or purchase third-party scanning licences.

Dynamic scanning is executed in a runtime environment and identifies vulnerabilities for containers running in test, QA, or production environments, making it possible to catch vulnerabilities introduced by software installed post-build as well as zero-day vulnerabilities. For dynamic (or runtime) container security, there is an array of options provided by third parties, from open0source solutions such as CNCF Falco to offerings through AWS container competency partners, including Aqua Security, Trend Micro, and Twistlock.

Once Applications are in production, verify that they remain vulnerability-free. An organization can also scan images using an application programmable interface (API) command, allowing it to set up periodic scans for running container images to ensure continued monitoring. ECR sends a notification when a scan is completed, and the results are available in the console and over the API.

3.4.4 Use Case

This use case shows scheduled re-scans of container images used in a production environment. For example, the individual is in a secop role, looking after several ECR repositories, and rather than manually scanning images and reviewing the detailed findings of the image scans, he or she may use a high-level overview and the ability to drill down on a per-repository basis. The sample setup consists of four lambda functions, providing an HTTP API for managing scan configurations and taking care of scheduling the image scans, as well as an S3 bucket for storing the scan configurations:

3.4.5 Auditing Configuration Management

Securely configuring an organization's cloud technology environment is a responsibility shared between the organization and AWS. The organization provides requirements for secure configuration settings and expects AWS to provide a mechanism to implement and regularly audit the configurations in place.

4

ENTERPRISE RISK MANAGEMENT FRAMEWORK

Risk management methodologies stems from the ERM framework. This is defined as an organization's ability to understand, control and articulate the nature and level of risks taken into account the business strategy, coupled with accountability for organizational risk. One of the main benefits of the ERM framework is an enhanced viewpoint and focus on risk management within the organization.

ERM addresses the following organizational questions:

- Should we pursue this initiative? This aligns with strategy, risk appetite, culture and ethics.
- Can we achieve this initiative? This aligns people, processes, structure and technological capabilities, i.e., operational risk.
- Did we accomplish this initiative? This is the assessment of expected results, continuous learning and a robust system of checks and balances.

ERM promotes strategies that assist organizations to holistically manage risk. ERM is a governance structure that provides a horizontal view of the risk disciplines and operational risks of an institution.

The elements of the ERM framework include the following:

4.1 Internal Environment

Management determines the philosophy regarding risk and establishes the level of risk the organization is willing to assume known as the risk appetite. The internal controls environment provides the basis of how risk and controls are assessed and managed by an organization. The importance of ERM is communicated by executive management throughout the organization.

DOI: 10.1201/9781003404354-4

4.2 Common Language Around Risk

The risk management approach must involve establishing common risk terminology with appropriate training and awareness of the terminology by stakeholders within the organization. A common definition of risk "is the potential for loss, or the diminished opportunity for gain, which can obstruct the achievement of an organization's business objectives". A common terminology will facilitate communication across business units:

- Risk is the possibility that an event will occur and adversely affect the achievement of objectives.
- Risk culture is the appearance of ERM and the attitude towards it that management conveys to the organization's personnel. Are management actions aligned with the implemented ERM strategies?" (COSO, 2020).

4.3 Risk Management Steering Committee

It is important to establish a senior management-level committee to provide oversight of the implementation of the ERM framework. In addition, the committee will help delineate roles, responsibilities and accountabilities as identified within the framework.

Roles and responsibilities: must be clearly defined and communicated throughout an organization.

Board of directors and CEO: have ultimate accountability for all risks. Risk management practices must be discussed periodically, and risk management-related policies must be reviewed and approved.

Senior management: is responsible for designing, implementing and maintaining an effective framework. In addition, senior managers should develop policies and procedures, establish and monitor the risk appetite level, and report regularly to the board of directors.

Business units: 1) promote a risk-aware culture, 2) identify, 3) assess, 4) measure, 5) monitor, 6) control and 7) report risks to senior management, 8) manage relevant risks within the framework established by senior management, and 9) ensure compliance with policies and procedures.

Support departments, i.e., legal, HR, information technology (IT): provide support to business units in developing and enforcing policies and procedures.

Internal audit & compliance: monitor and provide independent assurance of the effectiveness of the framework.

Risk management: coordinates the establishment of the framework and provides expertise.

4.4 Objective Setting

Objectives must exist before management can identify potential events affecting the achievement of organizational goals. ERM ensures that management has a process in place to set objectives and that the chosen objectives support, align and are consistent with an organization's mission and risk appetite.

4.5 ERM Methodology

Developing a methodology for the ERM framework should include definitions of key risk terms, descriptions of roles and responsibilities, and clear procedures for risk identification, assessment, measurement, mitigation, monitoring and reporting. The methodology should be expressed in a formally written document that comprises all the key business areas. The document should consider the organization's strategic direction and objectives and clearly outline its capacity to take risks and its tolerance of potential loss. In addition, the risk appetite level must be regularly reviewed and approved by the senior management and board of directors.

4.5.1 Risk Appetite

Risk appetite is the amount of risk, on a broad level, that an organization is willing to accept as it tries to achieve its goals and provide value to stakeholders. It reflects the ERM philosophy and in turn influences the organization's culture and operating style.

4.5.2 Risk Tolerance

Risk tolerance is the acceptable level of variation relative to the achievement of a specific objective and is often measured using the same units as the related objective. In setting risk tolerance, management considers the relative importance of the related objective and aligns risk tolerance with risk appetite to ensure that it operates within its risk appetite level.

4.5.3 Event Identification

Potential events from internal or external sources that might have an impact on the organization and affect the achievement of its objectives must be identified. Event identification includes distinguishing between events that represent risks, those that represent opportunities, and those that may represent both risks and opportunities.

4.5.4 Risk Assessment

The identified risks are analysed and associated with objectives that may be affected to form a basis for determining how they should be managed. Risks are assessed on both an inherent and a residual basis, and the assessment should consider both risk likelihood and impact. Risk assessment needs to be performed continuously and throughout an organization.

4.5.5 Quantitative Risk Assessment

Quantitative risk assessment refers to attempts to assign a monetary value to the assets being assessed, a monetary cost to the impact of an adverse event, and percentages to the frequency of threats and the likelihood of events.

4.5.6 Risk Calculation

Risk = Asset Value x Threat x Vulnerability
Asset value is usually the easiest to measure, however it is difficult to quantify certain assets, such as institutional reputation.

Threat, it may be very difficult to measure the potential for harm, although information from external sources is useful.

Vulnerability can be measured using an automated computing device vulnerability tools to provide information, but not all vulnerabilities can be quantified.

4.5.7 Qualitative Risk Assessment

Qualitative risk assessments are scenario driven and do not attempt to assign a monetary value to the assets being assessed or to the impact of an adverse event. They aim to rank the impacts of threats and criticality of assets into categories such as low, medium and high.

4.5.8 Risk Response

The organization identifies and evaluates possible responses to risks, which include avoiding, accepting, reducing and sharing risks. Management selects a set of actions to align risks with the organization's risk tolerance and risk appetite. The ERM framework advocates the following responses:

- Avoidance means the organization ceases the activities that cause the risk. Some examples of avoidance are ending a product line, selling a division, or deciding against expansion.
- Reduction means action is taken to mitigate the risk likelihood and impact.
- Sharing means reducing the risk likelihood and impact by sharing a portion of the risk. An extremely common sharing response is insurance.
- Acceptance means no action is taken to affect the risk likelihood or impact.

4.5.8.1 Control Activities Policies and procedures are established and implemented to ensure that the risk responses selected by management are effectively carried out.

4.5.8.2 Risk Identification Risk identification can be completed through a risk control self-assessment (RCSA) approach coordinated by risk management and conducted with subject-matter experts. This method uses a risk taxonomy to identify applicable risks, inherent risk levels, quality of internal controls and residual risk levels.

The process consists of the following steps:

- Identify applicable risks and describe the business activity that exposes the business unit to each risk.
- Establish the inherent risk level *(H, M, L)* and typical annual damage. Inherent risk prevents the achievement of business objectives without consideration of internal controls. Typical annual damage, if applicable, can be estimated based on the subjective judgement of the business unit and should include consideration of both past (actual losses) and potential future occurrences.
- Assess and rank the quality of internal controls *(H, M, L)* and the reason for the assessment. Internal controls mitigate the inherent risk and involve the implementation of policies, procedures and standards.
- Calculate the residual risk level *(H, M, L)* that remains after considering the relevant internal controls. For example, a medium inherent risk and low-quality internal controls will result in a high residual risk level.

4.5.9 Risk Prioritization

Using the results of the RCSA for each business unit, the key risks should be prioritized based on the residual risk levels. All high residual risks should be discussed with the risk management steering committee, and risk mitigation plans (RMPs) should be developed.

4.5.10 Risk Mitigation Plans

RMPs must be established by taking a risk-based approach to address areas with the greatest control weaknesses and largest potential for loss. Organizations will generally run out of resources before they run out of risk; therefore, high-risk items must be prioritized.

Completion dates should be targeted and responsible owners selected to facilitate the risk mitigation process.

4.5.11 Information and Communication

Relevant information is identified, captured and communicated in a form and time frame that enables people to carry out their responsibilities. Information for identifying, assessing and responding to risk is needed at all levels of an entity.

4.5.12 Monitoring

ERM is monitored, and modifications are made as necessary. In this way, the organization can react dynamically, changing as conditions warrant.

4.5.13 Risk Monitoring and Reporting

The key risks that were identified must be monitored and periodically reported to the senior management and board of directors.

4.6 Scenario Planning and Stress Testing

Among the many tools a manager can use for strategic analysis, scenario planning can capture a wide range of possibilities with specific details. By identifying fundamental trends, the technology executive can define a series of scenarios that will assist the organization in reducing errors in the decision-making process.

"Scenarios are thorough and probable views of how business environments might extend into the future" (Ringland, 2002).

4.6.1 Step 1: Brainstorm Future Scenarios

In the first step, the time frame is determined based on the following factors:

- The lifecycle of the product
- Political conditions within the country

- Competitor analysis
- Technological advancement

4.6.2 *Step 2: Identify Trends and Driving Forces*

Consider the following factors:

- Who has an interest in these decisions?
- Who will be affected by them?
- Who could influence them?

The apparent driving forces include but are not limited to suppliers, customers, competitors, employees, shareholders, and government. Identification of the following factors is also essential:

- Current roles of the driving forces
- Their interests
- Their positions in the field
- Their progress over time

4.6.3 *Step 3: Create a Scenario Planning Template*

The driving forces of the environment are identified from the key factors identified in Step 2. These driving forces can originate in the following areas:

- Society and its structures, including demographic, economic and political factors as well as public opinion.
- Markets and customer behaviour.
- Technology and innovation.
- The organization's competitive structure within its industry.
- The organization's organizational capacities and core competencies.

The forces that are highly predictable should be identified so that the organization can focus on the effects that are less likely to occur.

4.6.4 *Step 4: Develop a Scenario*

The essential task of scenario planning is developing the actual scenario. Through this phase, a situation should be built that incorporates each factor evaluated in the above steps and considers the traits and trends of the market. In building a scenario, the strengths and weaknesses of the plan should be identified and considered.

4.6.5 Step 5: Evaluate a Scenario

Through a systematic step-by-step procedure, the scenario team can achieve a balance between creativity and free-form imagination by using sound judgement based on knowledge and experience.

4.6.5.1 Scenario Analysis **Scenario analysis shows** a forward-looking view of operational **risk** that augments historical internal and external data. These exercises allow stakeholders to identify and **manage** the **risk** exposures through business decisions and **risk** mitigation strategies.

Threat actor analysis: Identify actors who pose a threat to the organization.

Impact analysis: Determine the areas that the organization is focused on protecting.

Scenario selection: Determine scenarios that could have a catastrophic impact on the organization.

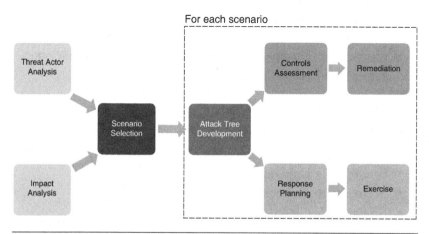

Figure 4.1   shows the process of scenario analysis.

At minimum, a scenario should include the following:

The situation: An explanation of the sequence of events that leads to an adverse outcome. These may be industry- and organization-specific but must include items such as

- Business Continuity Planning (BCP) events.
- External attacks by hackers, competitors or government agencies.
- Malicious insiders stealing information.
- Accidental release of confidential information.
- The mishandling of data by vendors and third parties.

The outcomes: Outcomes that are unfavourable to an organization and are a result of the event should be clearly identified. An event may have multiple outcomes, for example, the same scenario may result in the loss of revenue, legal costs and regulatory fines. Each outcome should be explicitly laid out and its impact described.

Controls in place: Controls work as separate lines of defence, at times sequentially and at other times interacting with each other to help prevent the occurrence of an adverse event. Often, the correct operation of one control may provide adequate protection or mitigation. If controls operate independently of each other, as they often do, the combined probability of all of them failing simultaneously tends to be significantly lower than the probability of any one of them failing.

Frequency of occurrence: The frequency or likelihood of the scenario being realized should be a part of the scenario analysis and is best estimated in a discussion with management.

Severity of the outcomes: The severity of each of the adverse outcomes should be estimated separately.

Scenario examples:

- Scenario #1: Patch management.
- Scenario #2: Network ransomware/malware attack.
- Scenario #3: Unplanned attack.
- Scenario #4: Financial break-in/external attack.
- Scenario #5: Cloud security breach.

Attack tree development: Develop detailed attack trees for each scenario.

Control assessment: Map controls to the attack tree and assess effectiveness.

Remediation: Use the control assessment to plan remediation projects that address control gaps.

Response planning: Create or enhance existing response plans to cater to extreme scenarios.

Exercise: Test the control strength, response plan and overall preparedness.

4.6.6 Step 6: Update Strategies and Policies Accordingly

A month or two after the scenarios are implemented, it is essential to evaluate the strategic plan and update the policies. This evaluation and update process should be completed on a periodic basis.

4.7 Operational Risk Management

Operational risk is defined by the Bank of International Settlements (BIS) as "the risk of loss resulting from inadequate or failed internal processes, people and systems or from external events (strategic and reputational risk is not included in this definition for the purpose of a minimum regulatory operational risk capital charge)", (Banking for International Settlement, 2001).

Legal risk is included in this definition. Operational risk is therefore the sum of operating, information systems, compliance and legal risk.

In addition to the responsibility to protect organizational assets from the threats that exist in the current environment, risk managers have the responsibility to consider and manage risks to individuals when information systems process sensitive information, i.e., PII.

4.8 Information Security Aspects of Operational Risk

"Security risk management provides a means of better understanding the nature of security threats and their interaction at an individual, organizational, or community level (Standards Australia, 2006, p. 6). Generically, the risk management process can be applied in the security risk management context. The risk management process advocated in ISO 31000 should be used as the foundation for risk management in an organization; however, security risk management has several unique processes that other forms of risk management do not consider."

The core of security risk management is identical to enterprise risk management that has been discussed in Chapter 2, with the addition of informational assessments, such as threat, criticality register and vulnerability assessment. Security risk management is the integration between risk management and these assessments forms:

4.9 Cybersecurity Risk Assessment Process

Information security risk management is the systematic application of management policies, procedures and practices to establish the context for information security risks and identifying, analysing, evaluating, treating, monitoring and communicating those risks.

ISO 27005 is the "Information Technology—Security Techniques—Information Security Risk Management" standard released by the International Organization for Standardization (ISO) to provide guidance for the information security risk management processes that are needed to implement an effective information security management system (ISMS). Although this standard is considered a risk management standard, a significant portion addresses information security risk assessments, which are a key part of a risk management program.

ISO 27005 is aligned with NIST SP 800–30 and is written from a high-level perspective compared to other frameworks. ISO 27005 has 5 major topic areas:

   i. Information security risk assessment
  ii. Information security risk treatment
 iii. Information security risk acceptance
 iv. Information security risk communication
  v. Information security risk monitoring and review

4.10 Risk Identification

Information security risk assesses the impacts that can occur on an organization and its stakeholders, due to the threats and vulnerabilities associated with the operation of its information systems and the environments in which those systems operate. The primary means of mitigating information security-related risk is to select, implement, maintain and continuously monitor preventative, detective and corrective security controls to protect information assets from compromise or to limit the damage to an organization should a compromise occur.

Risk identification consists of the following five main activities.

4.10.1 Identification of Assets

The objective for this activity is to identify the assets that are in the scope of the risk assessment, including identifying the asset owners. In ISO 27005, assets are categorized as either primary or secondary. Primary assets are core processes, activities and information and secondary assets are hardware, software, network, personnel, site and structure.

4.10.2 Identification of Threats

The objective of this step is to prepare a list of potential threats to each asset. According to ISO 27005, stakeholders such as asset owners, users, human resources staff and facilities management can assist in identifying these threats. ISO 27005 also states that internal experience, particularly based on previous incidents or assessments, should be considered. One of the most useful contributions of ISO 27005 is the inclusion of standardized threat catalogues.

4.10.3 Identification of Existing Controls

The objective of this activity is to identify existing controls. The guidance provided within ISO 27005 for this activity is open-ended and does not specifically address the criteria or scale of the control review.

ISO 27005 does provide references to information sources that may be able to assist in this activity. Examples of information sources for this part of the review are as follows:

- Documents that have information about controls.
- People responsible for information security.
- Onsite reviews.
- Review of internal audit results.

4.10.4 Identification of Vulnerabilities

The goal is to identify an asset's vulnerabilities through the following actions:

- Vulnerability scanning and penetration testing.
- Code reviews
- Interviews
- Questionnaires
- Physical inspection
- Document analysis

4.10.5 Identification of Consequences

The objective of this activity is to determine the possible damage or consequences that could be caused by an "incident scenario", or what other frameworks refer to as a threat scenario. ISO 27005 provides a list of impact factors that can be used to identify and measure consequences.

4.11 Expressing and Measuring Risk

Information security risk "is measured in terms of a combination of the likelihood of an event and its consequence".

It is further defined as an information security event, meaning "an identified occurrence of a system, service or network state indicating a possible breach of information security policy or failure of safeguards, or a previously unknown situation that may be security relevant".

In measuring risk, it is not the risk of a single, critical event that matters but the general map of risk composed of all possible critical events. This enables the assessor to determine the total risk, especially of probable events or especially severe events. There are two fundamental areas of risk that during analysis allow possible critical events to be classified according to their importance for the appropriate functioning of the organization. The first is operational security, and the second type is business continuity.

4.12 Risk Analysis

Risk analysis consists of the determination and evaluation of

- Processes that enable the realization of organizational tasks.
- Disruptive phenomena and the probability of their occurrence.
- Resource vulnerability in the sense of the magnitude of disruptive phenomena and their potential influence on organizational activity.

Risk analysis is a prerequisite for subsequently treating risk. Risk treatment pertains to controlling the risk so that it remains within acceptable levels. Risk can be reduced by applying security measures. Risk can also be

- Shared by outsourcing or insuring.
- Avoided
- Accepted, in the sense that the organization accepts the likely impact of a security incident.

The likelihood of a security incident occurring is a function of the likelihood that a threat will appear and that the threat will be able to successfully exploit the relevant system vulnerabilities. The consequences of the occurrence of a security incident are a function of the likely impact the incident will have on the organization as a result of the harm sustained by the organization's assets.

4.13 Risk Evaluation and Quantification

Risk evaluation is the process of comparing the results of the risk analysis with the risk evaluation criteria defined to determine whether the cyber-risks are acceptable. The following are the basic steps of the risk evaluation process:

- Identification
- Probability and impact
- Identified risk
- Treatment
- Secondary risk
- Residual risk
- Monitoring and review

Organization-wide security and privacy risk should be assessed, and the risk assessment results should be updated on an ongoing basis. There are two types of risk assessment:

- Qualitative
- Quantitative

4.14 Risk Mitigation Planning and Verification

Risk mitigation planning is the process of developing options and actions to enhance opportunities and reduce threats to project objectives. Risk mitigation implementation is the process of executing risk mitigation actions. Risk mitigation progress monitoring includes tracking identified risks, identifying new risks, and evaluating risk process effectiveness throughout the initiative.

The risk mitigation step involves the development of mitigation plans designed to either manage, eliminate or reduce risk to an acceptable level. Once a plan is implemented, it is continually monitored to assess its efficacy with the intent of revising the course of action if needed.

General guidelines for applying risk mitigation management options are based on the assessed combination of the probability of occurrence and the severity of the consequences of an identified risk.

4.15 Risk Treatment

Risk Modification

The introduction of an additional factor that can positively or negatively influence risk.

Risk Transfer

The identification of ways and means to transfer a risk, either through the acquisition of insurance (i.e., cyber insurance) or by outsourcing.

Risk Avoidance

Electing not to pursue a business activity that would cause the risk to appear.

Risk Acceptance

Conscious and deliberate acceptance of the identified level of risk, without any other alteration by way of modification or transference.

4.16 Risk Remediation

The selection of a range of tactics, techniques and procedures to reduce an asset's susceptibility to compromise.

4.17 Risk Communication

Risk communication is an important tool for disseminating information and improving understanding of risk management decisions. This understanding and information enable stakeholders to make informed decisions about how the decision will impact their interests and values.

4.18 Risk Monitoring and Review

Risk monitoring and review is the process of identifying, analysing and planning for newly discovered risks and managing identified risks. Throughout the process, the risk owners track identified risks, reveal new risks, implement risk response plans and gauge the effectiveness of risk response plans.

4.19 Loss Event Management

Understanding and managing loss events is essential to an effective operational risk management program. This process includes the frequency, amount, type and sources of loss events as well as a comprehensive list of loss events.

4.20 Security Metrics

Metrics can provide insights into information security program effectiveness, levels of regulatory compliance, and the ability of staff and departments to address security issues for which they are responsible. Metrics can also help identify levels of risk in not taking certain mitigation actions and thus provide guidance for prioritizing future resource investments. Because metrics provide concrete facts and a common vocabulary for communicating risks, they may additionally be used to raise the level of security awareness within the organization.

Security metrics are tools designed to facilitate decision-making and improve performance and accountability through collecting, analysing and reporting relevant performance-related data. IT security metrics are based on IT security performance goals and objectives.

Effective metrics are often referred to as SMART (specific, measurable, attainable, repeatable, and time dependent). These metrics should also indicate the degree to which security goals are achieved and facilitate actions to improve the organization's overall security program. It is important to consider the following:

- How difficult it might be to collect accurate data for a given metric.
- The potential that the metric might be misinterpreted.
- The need to periodically review metrics that are being tracked and make changes as needed.

4.20.1 Key Performance Indicators

A key performance indicator (KPI) is a measure of performance commonly used to help an organization define and evaluate how successful it is, typically in terms of making progress towards its long-term organizational goals.

Below are some examples of clear cybersecurity metrics that can be tracked and easily presented to the relevant stakeholders.

Level of preparedness: How many devices on an organization's network are fully patched and up to date?

Unidentified devices on the internal network: How many such devices are on an organization's network?

Intrusion attempts: How many times have attackers breached the organization's network?

Mean time to detect (MTTD): How long do security threats go unnoticed? MTTD measures how long it takes for an organization to become aware of a potential security incident.

Mean time to resolve (MTTR): How long does it take an organization to respond to a threat once it has been uncovered?

Days to patch: How long does it take an organization to implement security patches?

Cybersecurity awareness training results: Who has taken (and completed) training? Did they understand the material?

Number of cybersecurity incidents reported: Are users reporting cybersecurity issues to the organization?

Security ratings: Often, the easiest way to communicate metrics to non-technical colleagues is through an easy-to-understand scorecard.

4.20.2 Key Risk Indicators

A key risk indicator (KRI) is a measure used by management to indicate the risk associated with an activity. KRIs are metrics used by an organization to provide early signals of increasing risk exposure in various areas of the enterprise.

KRI examples

- Information security training completeness
- Policy exceptions/deviations
- Phishing campaign failure rate
- Outstanding audit findings
- Risk assessment ratings
- Patch coverage by system
- Incidents and events

- Breaches
- Vulnerabilities by criticality and age
- Account management

4.20.3 Risk Culture & Risk Behaviours

Risk culture is the system of values and behaviours present in an organization that shapes the risk decisions of management and employees. One element of risk culture is a common understanding of the organization and its business purpose.

The risk culture of an organization is likely to:

- Determine the degree to which the organization's policies are internalized by staff and exhibited in day-to-day behaviour.
- Determine staff response to threats or situations that fall outside well-prescribed operating guidelines.
- Influence the organization's reputation among regulators, clients and the broader market.

5

DevRiskOps

Chapter 5: Cybersecurity Risk Management Framework

5.1 Cyber Risk Investment Model

The cyber risk investment model is comprised of the following elements:

1. Technology Landscape
2. Data Classification
3. Risk Management Practices
4. Cost-Benefit Analysis for Cyber Security Measures
5. Business Objectives

5.1.1 Technology Landscape

The technology landscape is defined as the technology and information security measures in place within the enterprise architecture. This landscape is usually depicted through enterprise architecture artefacts that include but are not limited to the visual layout of the technology, system interfaces, communication channels, application portfolios, technology stack and security measures. This landscape extends from the on-premises environment to suppliers, service providers, agents and partners.

5.1.2 Data Classification

Data classification, in the context of cyber risk management, is the classification of data based on its level of impact on an organization and includes collection, use, disclosure and retention. Protection of data is based on the data classification level, i.e., public, internal use, confidential, or restricted. These levels define the type of safeguards

DOI: 10.1201/9781003404354-5

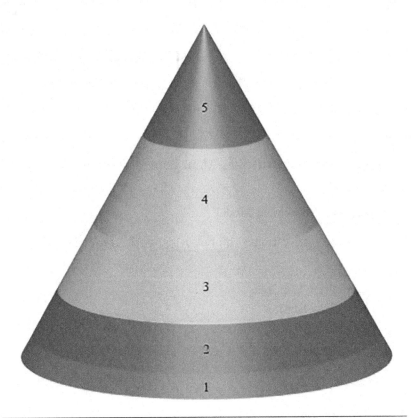

Figure 5.1   shows the cyber risk investment model, which comprises the 1) technology landscape and application portfolio, 2) data centric focus, 3) risk management practices, 4) cost-benefit analysis and 5) strategic development (Kissoon, 2020).

that should be in place to adequately protect the data, regardless of how they are stored. Protection of data includes safeguards to minimize loss, theft, unauthorized access, use, disclosure, copying and modification.

5.1.3 Risk Management Practices

All organizations are confronted with risks that have the potential to negatively affect their business. Risk management practices in the financial services sector focus on identifying, measuring and analysing those threats to reduce material, reputation, opportunity and other costs. These practices utilize the enterprise risk management (ERM) framework, which is integrated with information security, privacy risk, vulnerability management, system and application development lifecycle along with business continuity management (BCM).

5.1.4 Cost-Benefit Analysis for Cybersecurity Measures

Cost-benefit analysis is the widely accepted economic principle for managing all an organization's resources. This principle requires that the costs of an activity be compared to the benefits. When the benefits exceed the costs, it pays to engage in those activities, whereas if the costs exceed the benefits, the opposite is true. When the costs and benefits of an activity are equal, the decision-maker may factor other qualitative measures into the decision. The three major activities usually associated with cybersecurity are 1) protecting information from authorized users of the information, 2) making information available to authorized users on a timely basis, and 3) protecting information from integrity flaws.

5.1.5 Business Objectives

Business objectives are specific and measurable goals that an organization wants to attain as it focuses on growth, profitability, efficiency and stability. These objectives are interconnected with the enterprise strategy and appear directly within the business strategy and multi-year road map.

5.2 Integration of Risk Management Practices

Through 2015, 80% of the risks associated with attaining DevOps program objectives stemmed from how organizational change is managed.

The risk management process shows how to evaluate starting with the absence of internal controls, known as inherent risk. With the inclusion of proper certification of code, which indicates that the overall system works as intended, and that its environment protects it from undue influences, the risk is mitigated. Secure capabilities allow stakeholders to take pro-active actions such as quarantining, moving or deleting sensitive or non-public information from their network before it negatively impacts their capabilities through unauthorized exposure resulting in a risk to the business, I.e., brand, reputational, financial, legal, cybersecurity. Stakeholder should be empowered to:

- continuously monitor all networks and automate actions.
- discover, classify and act on all transactions involving data that has been identified as sensitive, business critical or confidential in order to have information privacy solutions.
- facilitate compliance with all laws and regulations that apply to data, users and transactions based on local and global laws as they apply.
- scale with information and footprint growth, and provide data protection in a timely and cost-effective manner that allows for predictable constant mission outcome.
- easily install, deploy and update in a reasonable timeframe to all appliances that are utilized by the University in a manner that does not cause interruption to end user expectation.
- minimize the need for IT oversight by creating automated pre-defined actions for information privacy solutions and data loss prevention.
- optimally, develop a data security and data privacy dashboard similar to and integrated with network management.
- provide daily, weekly, monthly and annual reports that can be used to satisfy audit requests.
- reduce business risk and liability.

A common reason used for not implementing DevOps and continuous delivery in IT organizations is that this approach does not comply with industry standards and regulations without considering the risk management process. Two controls that are often cited are segregation of duties and change management.

Regulations and standards require organizations to prove they know what is happening and why. Therefore, protecting information, services and performing accurate reporting is essential. Compliance with the authorities to acquire certain data and the mechanisms employed to secure the data acquired is at the forefront of many discussions today. Most IT organizations are subject to regulation and implement controls in order to ensure they comply. Controls are also essential to reducing the risk of loss that may affect the confidentiality, integrity, availability and privacy of information.

Leveraging a risk management approach, would facilitate an understanding of the residual risk, once internal controls are implemented. This would allow the business to gain an understanding of alignment of residual risk with the business unit's risk profile.

5.2.1 *Software Risk Management*

Risk denotes an uncertain event that will affect elements and may occur in some present or future process. In the context of software engineering, some additional definitions are made. Risk will be defined as a function of two parts: 1) the adverse impact an event would have if it occurred and, 2) the likelihood of the event occurring.

In order to further understand risk, it is essential to understand what is considered adverse events. These unfavourable events can be viewed from multiple levels of abstraction and can occur in different stages of maturity. The level of maturity is often split up in three terms: failure, error and bug. These terms are often erroneously believed to be interchangeable, but in the scope of risk management and software testing, they carry significantly different meanings.

- Failure is an externally observable malfunction of the program, in relation to specifications or expected behaviour.
- Error is a state of the program in which failures are possible.
- Fault, is the root cause (in the codebase or environment) of the error state and used interchangeably with" bugs", and" errors" with" faulty states".

The aim of software risk management is for an organization to have a framework implemented that covers work related to the risk associated with operations. The goal is to continuously identify, analyze, and assess the risk associated with a software project in a systematic, procedural manner. This can in many cases help mitigate the risk of adverse events and prepare responses for a situation in which one or several of the identified risks have occurred. There has been a substantial amount of research committed to unifying and standardizing the risk management work, both in the scope of software projects, and in more general terms. One study that is often referenced is the NIST SP 800–39 Risk Management Process. This states that there are four core activities that need to take place in an organization's risk management process for it to be sufficient. These activities and the information below flow necessary are outlined below:

1. Framing risk, this is the step where the context of the risk is defined, and where the potential risk factors are identified.
2. Assessing risk, this is the step where the probability and potential impact of a risk factor is examined.
3. Responding to risk, this is the step where it is decided how to react in case of an adverse event, and what to make of the assessed risk factors. Identifying risk has no inherent value, mitigating negative value imposed through response plans and risk avoidance is what results in value.
4. Monitoring risk, this is the process of monitoring the implementation, and effectiveness of the risk management plan decided upon through the other steps. This step is the continuous aspect of risk management and is responsible for spotting new risks, more efficient solutions and tracking.

5.2.2 Software Risk Assessment

Risk assessment is an essential part of any software development process that involves external parties, such as any production-grade project. There are many different definitions, and the codifying process is ongoing. There are, however, some general aspects that are agreed

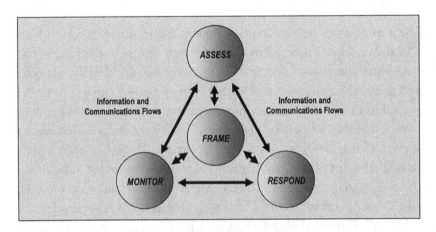

Figure 5.2 shows the elements of the risk management process (NIST, 2020).

upon. At its most basic, it is the process of gathering information related to the process or processes of interest, in order to assess the risks related to them. This often includes estimating both the likelihood that an event that would affect the project negatively would occur and estimating the extent to which the adversity would impact the project. It is a complex process that requires analyzing relevant data, both regarding the project specifically, and regarding the organization and potential end users. Risk models include: 1) Software risk assessment model (SRAM) and 2) Software Risk Assessment and Estimation Model (SRAEM).

5.2.2.1 Software Risk Assessment Model (SRAM) This model, appropriately called the Software Risk Assessment Model (SRAM), was one of the first efforts to provide a modeled flow for the risk assessment process. It identifies 9 critical risk elements, these are:

1. Complexity of Software
2. Staff Involved in the Project
3. Targeted Reliability
4. Product Requirements
5. Method of Estimation
6. Method of Monitoring
7. Development Process Adopted
8. Usability of Software
9. Tools used for Development

The model is based on a questionnaire, where a set of questions are formulated for each risk element. Each question can in turn be answered in one of three ways, in an increasing order of risk, such that a risk score between 1–3 can be given for that question. A normalized risk score is then calculated for each of these elements, by accumulating the numerical ratings and dividing it by the number of questions given for a question. This normalized value is called the risk element probability and shows what element carries the most risk, making it easier for decision makers to know where to allocate resources. The different elements can however have a varying degree of impact on a project. Thus, in order to calculate the overall risk of a project, the risk element probability needs to be weighted according to their potential impact.

5.2.2.2 Software Risk Assessment and Estimation Model (SRAEM)
Another model called the Software Risk Assessment and Estimation Model (SRAEM) focuses both on assessing risk as well as estimating it. The model assumes three key risk assessment dimensions, namely risk identification, risk analysis and risk prioritization. The risk identification process aims to identify and list the risk items for a specific project. Common methods for this are: examination of decision drivers, assumption analysis and checklists. The purpose of risk analysis is to assess the identified risks, in terms of their probability of occurrence and the magnitude of their impact. The commonly used techniques for this include performance models, cost models, and network analysis. Finally, the risk prioritization procedure should result in a ranked list of the risk items that have been identified and analyzed. The typical ways of doing this include risk exposure analysis and risk reduction leverage.

With most development projects, there is inherent risk in software development projects. Most of the software's fails are attributed to items such as budget overage and delay in the delivery of the software. The software risk assessment and estimation model (SRAEM) is used to predict the possible results of software projects with solid accuracy. The risk is estimated using risk exposure and software metrics of risk management and this metric is based on mission critical requirements stability risk metrics (MCRSRM). This software metrics is used when there are changes in requirements such as addition, subtraction or deletion. This model gives the incremental risk for every phase and the total cumulative risk as the software progress from phase to phase.

5.3 Cybersecurity Risk Management Framework

Risk assessment is an essential part of any organizational process, i.e., business, technology, software, and can involve external third parties, such as suppliers, agents and vendors. There are many different definitions, but at its most basic, it is the process of gathering information related to the process or processes of interest to assess the risks related to them. It often includes estimating both the likelihood that an event will negatively affect the organization, i.e., processes,

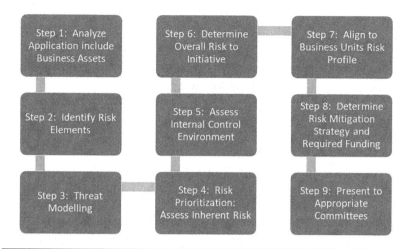

Figure 5.3 shows the cybersecurity risk management assessment process (Kissoon, 2020).

technology, and projects, and the extent to which that adversity will impact the organization. It is a complex process that requires analysing the relevant data related to the specific processes, technologies and projects, as well as the data related to the organization and potential end users.

5.4 Risk Assessment Process

The risk assessment process identifies critical risk elements, some examples are as follows:

1. Data classification.
2. Strategic/business requirements.
3. Application development.
4. Vendor relationships.
5. Technology landscape.
6. Legal/regulatory issues.
7. Brand/reputational issues.
8. Operational issues.
9. Financial issues.
10. Security and fraud issues.

5.4.1 Risk Prioritization: Assess the Inherent Risk

The risk assessment process is based on a questionnaire in which a set of questions is formulated for each risk element. Examples of the question categories include the following:

- Financial loss.
- Media attention.
- Reportable to Regulator.
- Impact to suppliers and employees.
- Loss or damage to Information Systems with very limited downtime.

Each question can be answered in one of five ways, in increasing order of risk, such that a risk score between 1 and 5 can be assigned for that question based on two rating scales, i.e., likelihood and impact. A quantitative inherent risk score can be calculated for each question, each risk element and the overall project, as follows:

- Risk score per question: product of the likelihood and impact rating.
- Risk score per element: accumulating the numerical score per question and dividing it by the number of questions for a risk element.
- Risk score for the overall initiative: accumulating the numerical score per risk element and dividing it by the number of risk elements in each project.

This quantitative inherent risk score is assigned a qualitative risk score categorized as high, medium or low. The qualitative inherent risk score shows which element carries the most risk, making it easier for decision-makers to decide where to allocate resources.

5.4.1.1 Impact Rating Scale The chart below shows the quantitative scale for the impact rating based on a score of 1–5

5.4.1.2 Likelihood Rating Scale The chart below shows the quantitative scale for the impact rating based on a score of 1–5

5.4.1.3 Qualitative Inherent Risk Rating The chart below shows the scale of the qualitative inherent risk rating based on the quantitative inherent risk score:

Table 5.1 shows a sample impact rating scale (Kissoon, 2020).

IMPACT	CRITERIA
Critical 5	• Financial loss of over $5 million. • International short-term negative media coverage with impact to market share. • Reportable to regulator and requires a corrective action plan and implementation dates. • Legal and regulatory impact to include the following: fees, fines, litigation, compliance enforcement, senior executive impact. • Significant Impact to suppliers and employees. • Significant loss or permanent damage to information systems; excessive downtime; over triple the expected RTO.
Major 4	• Financial loss of $1 million up to $5 million. • National short-term negative media coverage, potential to lose market share. • Reportable to regulator and requires a corrective action plan. • Some senior managers are impacted. • Impact on suppliers and employees. • Major loss or damage to information systems, continuous downtime, increase to expected RTO.
Moderate 3	• Financial loss of $500,00 up to $1 million • Short-term negative media coverage • Reportable to Regulator with potential of corrective plan to be provided • Minimal impact to suppliers and employees • Some loss or damage to Information Systems, intermittent downtime, possible to achieve expected RTO
Minor 2	• Financial loss of $100,000 up to $500,00. • No reputational damage. • No media attention. • No reportable incident to regulator. • Minimal impact to suppliers and employees. • Minimal loss or damage to information systems with minimal downtime.
Insignificant 1	• Financial loss up to $100,000. • No media attention. • Not reportable to Regulator. • No impact to suppliers and employees. • No significant loss or damage to information systems with very limited downtime.

5.4.2 Assess the Internal Controls

5.4.2.1 Internal Control Environment Control environment and monitoring activities are foundational for an organization to effectively manage its information security risk exposure.

Table 5.2 shows a sample likelihood rating scale, (Kissoon, 2020).

LIKELIHOOD	CRITERIA
Almost Certain **5**	• Almost certain. • Minimum of once in 6 months. • Greater than 90% chance of occurrence over the life of the asset or project.
Likely **4**	• Likely. • Minimum of once in 1 year. • 60% to 90% chance of occurrence over the life of the asset or project.
Possible **3**	• Possible. • Minimum of once in 5 years. • 30% to 60% chance of occurrence over the life of the asset or project.
Unlikely **2**	• Unlikely. • Minimum of once in 10 years. • 10% to 30% chance of occurrence over the life of the asset or project.
Rare **1**	• Rare. • Minimum of once in 20 years. • < 10% chance of occurrence over the life of the asset or project.

Table 5.3 shows a sample qualitative inherent risk rating scale, (Kissoon, 2020).

INHERENT RISK	QUANTITATIVE RISK CALCULATION
High	Range: 10+
Medium	Range: 4–10
Low	Range: 1–4

As stated in the *2013 COSO Framework*, "The control environment is the set of standards, processes, and structures that provide the basis for carrying out internal control across the organization. The board of directors and senior management establish the tone at the top regarding the importance of internal control and expected standards of conduct."

5.4.2.2 Cybersecurity and Privacy Risk Framework The privacy framework approach to privacy risk involves considering privacy events as potential problems individuals could experience that arise from system, product or service operations with data, whether in digital or non-digital form, through a complete lifecycle from data collection through disposal.

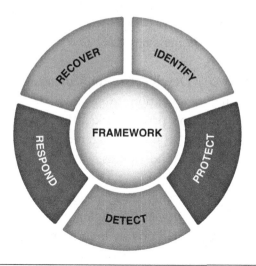

Figure 5.4 shows the NIST Cybersecurity Framework, (NIST, 2018).

5.4.2.3 Privacy Framework Functions The five privacy framework functions are defined as follows:

5.4.2.3.1 Identify-P Develop the organization's understanding of how to manage privacy risks for individuals arising from data processing. The activities in the identify-P function are foundational for the effective use of the Privacy Framework. Inventorying the circumstances under which data are processed, understanding the privacy interests of individuals who are directly or indirectly served or affected by the organization and conducting risk assessments, enable an organization to understand the business environment in which it is operating and identify and prioritize privacy risks.

5.4.2.3.2 Govern-P Develop and implement an organization's governance structure to enable an ongoing understanding of the risk management priorities that are informed by privacy risk. The govern-P function is similarly foundational but focuses on organization-level activities, for example 1) establishing the organization's privacy values and policies, 2) identifying legal/regulatory requirements, and 3) understanding the risk tolerance that enables the organization to focus and prioritize its efforts in ways that are consistent with its risk management strategy and business needs.

5.4.2.3.3 Control-P Develop and implement appropriate activities to enable the organization to manage data with sufficient granularity to understand privacy risks. The control-P function is associated with data processing management from the perspective of both organizations and individuals.

5.4.2.3.4 Protect P Develop and implement appropriate data processing safeguards. The protect-P function covers data protection to prevent cybersecurity-related privacy events and represents the intersection of privacy and cybersecurity risk management.

5.4.2.3.5 Communicate-P Develop and implement appropriate activities to enable the organization to have a reliable understanding of how data are processed and the associated privacy risks.

The communicate-P function includes the recognition that both the organization and individuals may need to know how data are processed to effectively manage privacy risks.

5.4.2.4 Privacy Risk Assessments Privacy risk management is a cross-organizational set of processes that assists the organization in understanding how its systems, products, and services may create concerns for individuals and how to develop effective solutions to manage these risks. *Privacy risk assessment* is a sub-process of identifying and evaluating specific privacy risks. In general, privacy risk assessments produce information that can assist organizations to weigh the benefits of data processing against the risks to determine the appropriate response.

The internal control environment is defined as the technology and information security controls in place within the enterprise architecture. This landscape is usually depicted through enterprise architecture artefacts, which include but are not limited to diagrams, interfaces, communication channels and application/technology portfolios. In addition, it extends from the on-premises environment to suppliers, service providers, agents and partners. Therefore, in addition to internal assessments, external third-party assurance reports are utilized to assist with the assessment of the internal control environment.

Cybersecurity Framework

Some organizations utilize cybersecurity risk-based frameworks to manage cybersecurity risk. The industry framework has been established through NIST and is composed of the following three parts: the framework core, the framework implementation tiers, and the framework profiles. Each framework component strengthens the integration between cybersecurity activities and business drivers.

The framework core is a set of cybersecurity activities, desired outcomes and applicable references that are common across critical infrastructure sectors. The core provides industry standards, guidelines and practices in a way that allows for communication of cybersecurity activities and outcomes from the executive level to the implementation/operations level.

The framework core consists of five concurrent and continuous functions—identify, protect, detect, respond, and recover. When considered as a whole, these functions provide a high-level strategic perspective on the lifecycle of an organization's management

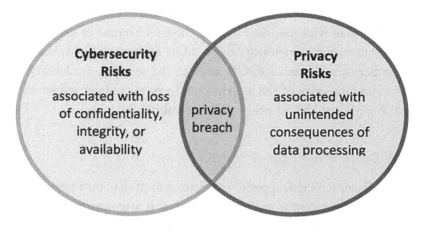

Figure 5.5   shows a cybersecurity and privacy risk relationship (NIST, 2019).

of cybersecurity risk through an assessment of the internal control environment. The framework core then identifies the underlying key categories and subcategories of the specific outcomes for each function. These outcomes are equated with informative references, such as existing standards, guidelines, and practices, for each subcategory.

5.4.2.5 Vendor Assurance Reports As outsourcing service providers (OSPs) manage a significant amount of customer data, systems, processes, and operations, their ability to manage associated risks while meeting increasing compliance requirements often emerges as a priority. Many service providers are reactive to third-party reporting due to the lack of full visibility in their reporting portfolios. Creating a library of enterprise-wide requirements and mapping individual obligations to corresponding controls can help identify gaps and overlaps. For example, an organization may have one control for regulating physical access to its data centre, but it may align with 20 different internal and external requirements. An integrated library of requirements and control tests can make it easier to compile customer-centric reports.

Outsourcing is a growing trend, and companies increasingly depend on third-party providers to deliver critical services. The purpose of third-party reports, i.e., SOC2 or ISAE3402 reviews, is to provide client auditors with an objective report that expresses an opinion about the control environment of a service organization. These reports are designed to provide assurances about the effectiveness of the controls in place at a service organization, i.e., SOC for Service Organizations: Trust Services Criteria (SOC2) assesses the security, availability, or processing integrity of the system used to process client information or the confidentiality or privacy of that information.

5.4.3 Determine the Organizational Risk Appetite

An organization's risk appetite is the amount of risk, on a broad level, that an organization is willing to accept as it attempts to achieve its goals and provide value to its stakeholders.

During the risk assessment process, an organization's residual risk is assessed to determine the remaining risk after internal controls are implemented.

Assessing this risk shows the organization the areas where a gap or lack of internal control exists. Usually, this is the area of focus for key stakeholders as they determine the cost-benefit analysis and risk mitigation strategy. In essence, residual risk should be aligned with the organization's/business unit's risk profile within the risk tolerance level.

Specifically, the residual risk score is a qualitative score that is more granular than the score of inherent risk. The inherent risk is assigned one of three scores, i.e., high, medium or low, while the residual risk is commonly assessed based on five or more possible scores, i.e., high, medium-high, medium, medium-low and low. This granularity highlights the control implementation progress over time and better reflects changes in overall risk.

5.4.4 Risk Mitigation Strategy

In some circumstances, to align the residual risk with the organization's/business unit's risk appetite, further mitigation is required. Therefore, organizations are required to make decisions about funding cybersecurity activities in a manner consistent with the viewpoints of various stakeholders. Below is a risk treatment scale, which aligns the impact, likelihood and inherent risk rating scale to identify areas that may require governance and risk mitigation through senior management oversight and additional cybersecurity measures.

Cost-benefit analysis is the widely accepted economic principle for managing an organization's resources. This principle requires that the costs of an activity be compared to the benefits. When the benefits exceed the costs, it pays to engage in those activities, whereas if the costs exceed the benefits, the opposite is true. When the costs and benefits of an activity are equal, the decision-maker may factor other qualitative measures into the decision.

The three major activities usually associated with cybersecurity are 1) protecting the information of the authorized users of the information, 2) making information available to the authorized users on a timely basis, and 3) protecting information from integrity flaws.

The costs associated with these activities are significant, as organizations will incur costs to detect and correct security breaches that cannot be prevented. The benefits of cybersecurity are related to the

Table 5.4 shows a sample risk treatment scale (Queensland Treasury and Trade, 2011).

LIKELIHOOD	IMPACT				
	INSIGNIFICANT	MINOR	MODERATE	MAJOR	CRITICAL
Rare	LOW: accept the risk, routine management	LOW: accept the risk, routine management	LOW: accept the risk, routine management	MEDIUM: specific accountability, risk mitigation plan	HIGH: quarterly senior management review
Unlikely	LOW: accept the risk, routine management	LOW: accept the risk, routine management	MEDIUM: specific accountability, risk mitigation plan	MEDIUM: specific accountability, risk mitigation plan	HIGH: quarterly senior management review
Possible	LOW: accept the risk, routine management	MEDIUM: specific accountability, risk mitigation plan	MEDIUM: specific accountability, risk mitigation plan	HIGH: quarterly senior management review	HIGH: quarterly senior management review
Likely	MEDIUM: specific accountability, risk mitigation plan	MEDIUM: specific accountability, risk mitigation plan	HIGH: quarterly senior management review	HIGH: quarterly senior management review	EXTREME: monthly senior management review
Almost Certain	MEDIUM: specific accountability, risk mitigation plan	MEDIUM: specific accountability, risk mitigation plan	HIGH: quarterly senior management review	EXTREME: monthly senior management review	EXTREME: monthly senior management review

cost savings, known as cost avoidance, associated with preventing cybersecurity breaches. The cost-benefit framework states that the goal of an organization should be to implement security procedures up to a point where the benefits minus the costs are maximized. In this framework, implementing cybersecurity activities beyond that point means that the incremental costs are greater than the incremental benefits of the additional security measures. In essence, the net benefit of implementing incremental cybersecurity measures beyond the maximum point is negative and, therefore, represents a financial cost to the organization.

In contrast, the cybersecurity risk management framework has four areas of consideration, as follows: 1) alignment with the organization's risk appetite, 2) alignment with the risk assessment process, 3) understanding of the cost-benefit analysis and 4) justification of the risk mitigation strategy. Although cost-benefit analysis is impactful from a financial perspective, in some cases, other factors need to be considered to fully understand the impact of not implementing additional security measures. Incurring the cost of preventative security measures is essential, as in most cost-benefit analyses, the actual cost of remediating a cybersecurity breach is unrealized. Specifically, most organizations do not have the data to appropriately access the cost/impact of a cybersecurity breach on an organization, such as its effect on the organization's brand/reputation, legal/regulatory landscape, operational/technology environment, forensic/e-discovery-related items, and third-party suppliers. Therefore, to adequately implement cybersecurity measures, in addition to conducting a cost-benefit analysis, stakeholders should implement an elaborate decision-making process to determine the additional security measures needed to adequately protect an organization from a cybersecurity breach while aligning with its risk appetite.

6

CASE STUDY

6.1 Case Study: Cascade Software

ABC University (ABC) is a semi-virtual organization, learners, staff and other stakeholder groups are reliant upon user interfaces (websites) to access online information and resources, i.e., courses, programs, and services. The usability and effectiveness of these interfaces, including the quality of their digital content, are paramount in establishing an effective digital experience. However, the university's current digital experience has become increasingly fragmented. In addition, the web publishing functionality in its existing solution (Alfresco Web Content Management) is no longer offered or supported by the vendor, and a scalable cloud-based solution is required to support the achievement of the university's strategic goals.

This risk assessment was intended to review the changes to content management and content delivery functions associated with the Cascade initiative. Any existing processes would be out of scope for this assessment, which included but was not limited to the identity and access management process that utilized the university's single sign-on (SSO) authentication mechanism. It is important to note that sensitive data are not intentionally stored within the CMS hosting architecture.

The Cascade initiative would perform the following:

o Implement a new DX platform and DNS server in ABC's cloud for internet and intranet publishing requirements.

DOI: 10.1201/9781003404354-6

o Develop a new scalable and high-availability architecture for ABC's internet and intranet, including a monitoring mechanism to gauge performance.

o Develop an internet and intranet site redesign and implementation plan that includes approaches to audit existing sites, develop criteria to identify "high-value sites", develop and implement SEO tactics, and work with stakeholders to redesign and deploy (or decommission and archive) primary sites based on the new web design and publishing standards and workflows.

o Integrate website improvement and digital asset management (DAM) tools with the DX platform via APIs and configuration.

o Rationalize and classify all identified sites.

o Redesign and deploy new sites deemed "high-value" primary sites and decommission and/or archive the old sites.

o Develop a list of secondary and tertiary sites for future redesign and deployment with the redesign of secondary and tertiary sites being out of scope.

o Establish analytics, i.e., Google Analytics, for all primary websites deployed.

The application has two components, i.e., content management and content delivery. The former is a publishing engine that distributes content to a user-defined target. The latter is an arbitrary solution that is utilized by the Cascade software product to provide web content to an audience that is most appropriate to the business.

The websites are categorized based on a criticality rating:

o Critical—medium volume (10,000+), tied to event or business process or important communications asset.

o Important—low-volume (<10,000) occasional use, not critical to move and can wait.

o Non-critical—faculty web content for current students and staff.

o LSS—low volume does not support a business process; however, it may contain historical information.

o Out of scope—high volume (50,000+) used daily—students and staff.

The Cascade web content management system provides a means to publish information about ABC University's academic resources for students and faculty and employment resources for staff. University websites are the primary means for communication with the audience; therefore, this is a business-critical application. The following services for website indexing, site search capabilities and DAM were included within this project:

1. SiteSearch360—Batman Option as an alternative to the Google Mini Search Appliance. The owner of this service is SEMKNOX GmbH, and it involves the insertion of simple JavaScript into the Cascade website to facilitate search capabilities, specifically 4 lines of code. Therefore, hosting or vendor involvement is out of scope.

   SiteSearch 360 has attained various industry requirements, as follows:

   o Payment card industry (PCI) data security standards (DSS) compliance.

   o ISO/IEC 27001:2013 for data centre certification.

   o The data processing agreement (DPA) required by general data protection regulations (GDPR).

   o Technical and organizational measures from SEMKNOX GmbH, the legal entity behind Site Search 360, and Hoster.

2. The Enterprise DAM solution utilizes an outsourced data centre managed by Brandfolder, and its features include the ability to perform the following:

   o Tag and categorize assets.

   o Manage asset metadata, i.e., name, date, and description.

   o Create a workflow, i.e., permissions for internal and external audiences, reviews and approvals, and notification.

   o Implement version control and rights management, i.e., user restrictions.

   o Implement asset sharing across various teams, i.e., lightboxes and asset tracking.

   o Perform searches, i.e., simple and advanced searches in the DAM.

   o Edit assets, i.e., images within the DAM, and convert to different formats.

o Replace an asset in the DAM and have the replacement changed on the website.
o Create a gallery within the DAM.
o Implement reporting.

The university does not intentionally store sensitive or classified information on the web content management system. However, the possibility of accidental storage and distribution of this type of information exists.

6.1.1 Questions

1. Determine the inherent risk.
2. Assess the internal control environment using the NIST Cybersecurity Framework: Core Components.
3. Determine the risk appetite, risk tolerance and risk profile.
4. Assess the residual risk and provide recommendations, if appropriate.
5. Develop the risk mitigation strategy.

6.2 Case Study: Cascade Software—Sample Report with Answers to Discussion Questions

6.2.1 Executive Summary

As a semi-virtual organization ABC learners, staff, and other stakeholder groups are reliant upon user interfaces (web sites) to access their online information and resources, i.e., courses, programs, services. The usability and effectiveness of these interfaces including the quality of their digital content are paramount to establishing an effective digital experience. However, ABC's current digital experience has become increasingly fragmented. In addition, the web publishing functionality in ABC's existing solution (Alfresco Web Content Management) is no longer offered or supported by the vendor and a scalable cloud-based solution is required to support achievement of ABC's strategic goals. This risk assessment will review the changes to content management and content delivery functions associated with the Cascade Project. Any existing processes will be out of scope for this assessment, this includes but not limited to the identity and access management process which utilizes the University's single sign on (SSO) authentication mechanism. It is important to note that sensitive data is not intentionally stored within the Hosting Architecture.

6.2.2 Business Impact and Risk

The business impact of the loss, disclosure or inappropriate use or modification of these websites can be legal, regulatory, or reputational in nature leading to significant financial and operational costs.

Business risk includes:

- Reputation Risk: Loss of customer confidence.
- Brand Risk: Unflattering or negative publicity due to press coverage which damages the University's brand.
- Operational Risk: Loss of operations and use of website by ABC users.
- Legal Risk: Fines and penalties assessed by regulators.
- Financial Risk: Significant costs to restore/repair any damages caused by intentional and unintentional users.

6.2.3 Results

In conclusion, the Hosting Architecture utilized by the Cascade Project has a **HIGHLY EFFECTIVE** control environment managed by ABC University in collaboration with Amazon Web Services (AWS). Although the inherent risk rating demonstrates a **MEDIUM** risk for the Hosting Architecture within the Cascade project, controls are in place resulting in a **LOW** residual risk rating for this initiative. The residual risk scale is in the Appendix.

6.3 Recommendations

Further risk mitigation can be utilized to include the following recommendations:

1. Data input and output integrity routines should be implemented for application interfaces and databases to prevent manual or systematic processing errors, corruption of data, or misuse.

2. Documentation should associate business roles with application roles or describe specific use cases for managing data within the application.

3. ABC should integrate customized vendor requirements into the University's security incident response plans.

4. ABC University should ensure that Vendors are routinely assessed using audits, test results or other forms of evaluations to confirm they are meeting their contractual obligations.

5. ABC University should ensure that response, recovery planning and testing are conducted with suppliers and third-party providers.

6. Existing technology and processes within ABC University should be reviewed and appropriate security controls implemented to include integration with ABC University's Active Directory.

7. The web-based interface should support authentication, including standards-based single-sign-on, leveraging multi-factor authentication and password/passphrase aging requirements.

8. ABC University should consider implementing an approved disaster recovery process to include Vendors.

9. ABC should ensure the following services are securely implemented with AWS:

   a. Infrastructure Services: Services such as Amazon Elastic Compute Cloud (Amazon EC2) and Amazon Virtual Private Cloud (Amazon VPC) are categorized as Infrastructure Services and, as such, require ABC to perform the necessary security configuration and management tasks. If the University deploys an Amazon EC2 instance, ABC is responsible for management of the guest operating system (including updates and security patches), any application software or utilities installed by ABC on the instances, and the configuration of the AWS-provided firewall (called a security group) on each instance.

   b. Container Services: The University is responsible for setting up and managing network controls, such as firewall rules, and for managing platform-level identity and access management separately from IAM. Examples of container services include Amazon Relational Database Services (Amazon RDS), Amazon Elastic Map Reduce (Amazon EMR) and AWS Elastic Beanstalk.

c. <u>Abstracted Services:</u> This category includes high-level storage, database, and messaging services, such as Amazon Simple Storage Service (Amazon S3), Amazon Glacier, Amazon DynamoDB, Amazon Simple Queuing Service (Amazon SQS), and Amazon Simple Email Service (Amazon SES). ABC accesses the endpoints of these abstracted services using AWS APIs and is required to ensure the connections are adequately protected.

d. <u>Security Incident Management:</u> The ability to monitor for intrusions within the AWS environment. In addition, AWS security/data related breach policies and procedures should be integrated with ABC University's incident management process.

6.3.1 Overview*

The Cascade project will:

o Implement a new DX platform and DNS server in ABC's cloud for ABC's internet and intranet publishing requirements.

o Develop a new scalable and high-availability architecture for ABC's internet and intranet including monitoring mechanism to gauge performance.

o Develop an internet and intranet site redesign and implementation plan that includes the approach to audit existing sites, develop criteria to identify "high-value sites", develop and implement search engine optimization (SEO) tactics, and to work with stakeholders to redesign and deploy (or decommission and archive) primary sites based on the new web design and publishing standards and workflows.

o Integrate web site improvement and digital asset management tools with the DX platform, via APIs and configuration.

o Rationalize and classify all identified sites.

o Redesign and deploy new sites deemed "high-value" primary sites and decommission and/or archive their old sites.

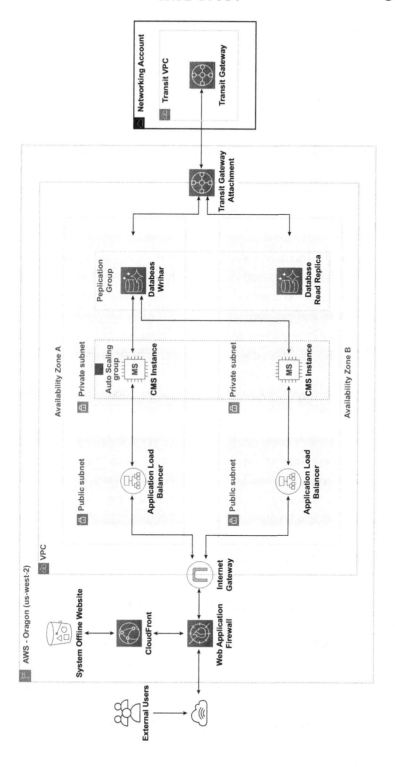

o Develop a list of secondary and tertiary sites for future redesign and deployment with the redesign of secondary and tertiary sites being out of scope.

o Establish analytics, i.e. Google Analytics for all primary web sites deployed.

The application has two components: content management and content delivery. The former is a publishing engine that distributes content to a user-defined target. The latter is an arbitrary solution that is utilized by the Cascade software product to serve web content to an audience that is most appropriate to the business.

The websites are categorized based on a criticality rating:

- Critical—medium volume (10,000+), tied to event or business process or important comms asset.
- Important—low volume (<10,000) occasional use, not critical to move and can wait.
- Non-critical—faculty web content for current students and staff.
- LSS- low volume does not support a business process, however, may contain historic information.
- Out of scope—high volume (50,00+) used daily—students and staff.

The Cascade web content management system provides a means to publish information about ABC University's academic resources for students, faculty, and employment resources for staff. University websites are the primary means for communication with its audience, therefore this is a business-critical application. The following services for website indexing, site search capabilities and digital asset management are included within this project:

1. SiteSearch360—Batman Option as an alternative to the Google Mini Search Appliance. The owners of this service are SEMKNOX GmbH, and this involves insertion of simple JavaScript into the Cascade website to facilitate search capabilities, specifically 4 lines of code, therefore hosting or vendor involvement is out of scope. SiteSearch 360 has attained various industry requirements:

   o Payment Card Industry (PCI) Data Security Standards (DSS) Compliance.

- o ISO/IEC 27001:2013 for their Datacenter Certification.
- o Data Processing Agreement (DPA) required by General Data Protection Regulations (GDPR).
- o Technical and Organizational measures from SEMKNOX GmbH, the legal entity behind Site Search 360, and Hoster.

2. The Enterprise Digital Asset Management solution utilizes an outsourced data center managed by Brandfolder, features include the ability to:

- o tag and categorize assets.
- o manage asset metadata, i.e. name, date, description.
- o create a workflow, i.e. permissions for internal and external audiences, reviews and approvals, notification.
- o implement version control, rights management i.e. user restrictions.
- o implement asset sharing across various teams, i.e. light-boxes and asset tracking.
- o perform search, i.e. simple and advanced search in the DAM.
- o edit asset, i.e. images within the DAM and convert to different formats.
- o replace an asset in the DAM and have the replacement changed on the website.
- o create a gallery within the DAM.
- o implement reporting.

The university does not intentionally store sensitive or classified information on the web content management system. However, the possibility exists for accidental storage and distribution of this type of information.

6.3.2 *Risk Assessment*

6.3.2.1 Impact and Likelihood   The impact and likelihood rating scale outlines the evaluation of the protection requirement level for each protection requirement. The table below shows the impact and likelihood rating as it applies to the risk elements.

	RISK ELEMENT	IMPACT	LIKELIHOOD
1	Data Classification PII: The university does not intentionally store sensitive or classified information on the web content management system. However, the possibility exists for accidental storage and distribution of this type of information.	Insignificant	Rare
2	Business Requirements Changes to content management and content delivery functions associated with the Cascade Project.	Critical	Unlikely
3	Application Development Application development includes a significant number of ABC's external websites to include hosting by Amazon Web Services (AWS)	Moderate	Possible
4	Vendor Relationship ABC has the following vendor relationships: AWS, Site Search 360 and Enterprise Digital Asset Management.	Critical	Possible
5	Technology landscape The technology landscape is a combination of the internal ABC's network, AWS and vendor data centers (Brandfolder).	Major	Likely
6	Legal/regulatory Disclosure of data subject to specific regulatory requirement.	Major	Possible
7	Brand/reputational Unflattering or negative publicity due to press coverage which damages ABC's brand. Loss of customer confidence due to the release or compromise of data.	Moderate	Possible
8	Operational Loss of operations and use of system by authorized users.	Moderate	Likely
9	Financial Significant costs to restore/repair any damages caused by intentional/unintentional users.	Minor	Possible
10	Security and fraud issues Loss and/or manipulation of sensitive data, i.e. disclosure of authentication credentials, distributed denial of service attack, malware attack, injection of malicious code.	Minor	Possible

6.4 Inherent Risk

The inherent risk rating for this application is medium, details to support this rating is in located in Chapter 5:

	RISK ELEMENT	QUANITATIVE INHERENT RISK RATING			QUALITATIVE INHERENT RISK RATING
		Impact	Likelihood	Rating	
1	Data Classification	1	1	1	Low
2	Business Requirements	5	2	10	Medium
3	Application Development	3	3	9	Medium
4	Vendor Relationship	5	3	15	High
5	Technology Landscape	4	4	16	High
6	Legal/regulatory	4	3	12	High
7	Brand/reputational	3	3	9	Medium
8	Operational	3	4	12	High
9	Financial	2	3	6	Medium
10	Security and fraud issues	2	3	6	Medium
	Average			9.6	Medium

6.5 Internal Control Assessment: Highly Effective

The following activities were completed to adequately assess the Hosting Architecture supporting the Cascade project, specifically:

1. Hosting Architecture—a CSA Consensus Assessments Initiative Questionnaire (CAIQ) was completed by ABC and AWS, along with AWS SOC for Service Organizations: Trust Services Criteria (SOC2, Type II) Report for the period October 1, 2019 to March 31, 2020.
2. Cascade Website(s)—a web application penetration test was completed by Digital Boundary Group (DBG).
3. Enterprise Digital Asset Management (DAM)—A SOC for Service Organizations: Trust Services Criteria (SOC2, Type II) Report was provided for the Brandfolder data center for the period March 1, 2019 to February 29, 2020.

6.6 Organization's Risk Appetite

The residual risk is a **LOW** rating for the Hosting Architecture within the Cascade project.

6.6.1 Risk Mitigation Strategy

Further risk mitigation recommendations can be utilized to align the organization's risk profile with the NIST Cybersecurity Framework core components. This area is essential as it provides recommendations to include additional cybersecurity measures that may provide a preventative approach. This would strengthen a risk-taking organization's risk profile without requiring the organization to transition to a risk averse profile. It is important to note that recommendations are not mandatory, and are used to identify additional cybersecurity measures to strengthen the organization's security posture while aligning with the organization's risk appetite.

6.6.2 Recommendations

6.6.2.1 Supplier Chain Risk Management

- ABC University should ensure that Vendors are routinely assessed using audits, test results or other forms of evaluations to confirm they are meeting their contractual obligations.
- ABC University should ensure that response, recovery planning and testing are conducted with suppliers and third-party providers.

6.6.3 Identity Management, Authentication and Access Control

- Existing technology and processes within ABC University should be reviewed and appropriate security controls implemented to include integration with ABC University's Active Directory.
- The web-based interface should support authentication, including standards-based single-sign-on, leveraging multi-factor authentication and password/passphrase aging requirements.

6.6.4 Information Protection Processes and Procedures

- ABC University should consider implementing an approved disaster recovery process to include Vendors.

6.6.5 Security Monitoring

- The ability to monitor for intrusions within the AWS environment.
- Integrate security/data related breach policies and procedures with ABC University's incident management process.

References

Alali, M., Almogren, A., Hassan, M. M., Rassan, I. A. L. & Bhuiyan, M. Z. A. 2017. Improving risk assessment model of cyber security using fuzzy logic inference system. *Computer & Security*, Online.

Albrechtsen, E. & Howden, J. 2009. The information security digital divide between information security managers and users. *Computer Security*, 28, 476–490.

Alexiou, S. 2019. Practical patch management and mitigation. *ISACA*, 3.

Alkaabi, A. 2014. *Strategic framework to minimize information security risks in the UAE*. PhD, University of Bedfordshire.

Avgerou, C. 2000. Information systems: What sort of science is it? *Omega (WestPort)*, 28, 567–579.

Bang, S. K., Chung, S., Choh, Y. & Dupuis, M. *A grounded theory analysis of modern web applications: Knowledge, skills, and abilities for DevOps*. Tacoma: Information Technology & Systems, Institute of Technology, University of Washington.

Baranyi, J. & Buss Da Silva, N. 2017. The use of predictive models to optimize risk of decisions. *International Journal of Food Microbiology*, 240, 19–23.

Basel Committee on Banking Supervision. 2001. *Operational risk, banking for international settlement*.

Battina, D. 2017. Best practices for ensuring security in Devops: A case study approach. *International Journal of Innovation in Engineering Research and Technology*, 4(11).

Bin Ishaq Alseiari, K. 2015. *The management of risk awareness in relation to information technology (MERIT)*. PhD, University of Gloucestershire.

Birks, M. & Mills, J. 2015. *Grounded theory: A practical guide*. London, UK: SAGE Publication.

Bojanc, R. & Jerman-Blazic, B. 2008. An economic modelling approach to information security risk management. *International Journal of Information Management*, 28, 413–422.

Bojanc, R., Jerman-Blažič, B. & Tekavčič, M. 2012. Managing the investment in information security technology by use of a quantitative modelling. *Information Processing & Management*, 48, 1031–1052.

Borgonovo, E., Cappelli, V., Maccheroni, F. & Marinacci, M. 2018. Risk analysis and decision theory: A bridge. *European Journal of Operational Research*, 264, 280–293.

Campos, J., Sharma, P., Jantunen, E., Baglee, D., Fumagalli, L. & Slotwiner, D. J. 2016. The challenges of cybersecurity frameworks to protect data required for the development of advanced maintenance. *Product-Service Systems across Life Cycle, Procedia*, 222–227.

Caralli, R., Stevens, J., Young, L. & Wilson, W. 2007. *Introducing OCTAVE allegro: Improving the information security risk assessment process.* Carnegie Mellon, USA.

Carty, M., Pimont, V. & Schmid, D. 2012. *Measuring the value of information security investments.* IT@Intel White Paper.

Cavusoglu, H., Mishra, B. & Ragunathan, S. 2004. A model for evaluating IT security investments. *ACM*, 47, 87–92.

Cavusoglu, H., Raghunathan, S. & Raghunathan, W. 2008. Decision-theoretic and game-theoretic approaches to IT security investment. *Management Information System*, 25, 281–304.

Cherdantseva, Y., Hilton, J., Rana, O. & Ivins, W. 2016. A multifaceted evaluation of the reference model of information assurance & security. *Computer & Security*, 63, 45–66.

Cho, S. 2003. *Risk analysis and management for information security.* PhD, Royal Holloway, University of London.

Claps, G., Svensson, R. & Aurum, A. 2015. On the journey to continuous deployment: Technical and social challenges along the way. *Information and Software Technology*, 21–31.

Comes, T., Hiete, M., Wijngaards, N. & Schultmann, F. 2011. Decision maps: A framework for multi criteria decision support under severe uncertainty. *Decision Support System*, 52, 108–118.

Committee of Sponsoring Organizations of the Treadway Commission. Viewed March 2020. www.coso.org.

Cremonini, M. & Nizovtsev, D. 2006. *Understanding and influencing attackers' decisions: Implications for security investment strategies.* Presented at the Workshop on the Economics of Information Security, June 26–28. Cambridge, England.

De Bruijn, H. & Janssen, M. 2017. Building cybersecurity awareness: The need for evidence-based framing strategies. *Government Information Quarterly*, 34, 1–7.

Dildy, T. 2017. Enterprise vulnerability management. *ISACA*, 2.

Dor, D. & Elovici, Y. 2016. A model of the information security investment decision-making process. *Computer & Security*, 63, 1–13.

Dresner, D. G. 2011. *A study of standards and the mitigation of risk in information systems*. PhD, University of Manchester.

Dutta, A. & McCrohan, K. 2002. Management's role in information security in a cyber economy. *California Management*, 45, 67–87.

Easterby-Smith, M., Thorpe, R. & Jackson, P. R. 2015. *Management & business research*. London, England: Sage.

Ericson, C. A. I. 2005. *Hazard analysis techniques for system safety*. John Wiley & Sons.

European Union Agency for Networks and Information Security, Octave v2.0. Viewed May 2020. www.enisa.europa.eu.

Farroha, B. S. & Farroha, D. L. 2014. A framework for managing mission needs, compliance and trust in the DevOps environment. *2014 IEEE Military Communications Conference*.

Fazlida, M. R. & Said, J. 2015. Information security: Risk, governance and implementation setback. *Procedia Economics and Finance*, 28, 243–248.

Feng, N., Wang, H. J. & Li, M. 2014. A security risk analysis model for information systems causal relationships of risk factors and vulnerability propagation analysis. *Information Science*, 256, 57–73.

Fiegenbaum, A. & Thomas, H. 1988. Attitudes toward risk and the risk-return paradox: Prospect theory explanations. *Academy of Management Journal*, 32, 85–106.

Fielder, A., Panaousis, E., Malacaria, P., Hankin, C. & Smeraldi, F. 2013. Decision support approaches for cyber security investment. *Decision Support Systems*, 86, 13–23.

Finne, T. 1998. A conceptual framework for information security management. *Computers & Security*.

Gabriela Roldán-Molina, A. B., Almache-Cueva, M., Silva-Rabadão, C., Yevseyeva, I., Basto-Fernandes, V. & Yevseyeva, C. V. B.-F. 2017. A comparison of cybersecurity risk analysis tools. *Centeris—International Conferences on Enterprise Information Systems*. Barcelona, Spain. Procedia Computer Science, 568–575.

Garvey, P. R. 2008. *Analytical methods for risk management: A systems engineering perspective*. Boca Raton, London, New York: Chapman-Hall/CRC-Press, Taylor & Francis Group (UK).

Ge, X.-Y., Yuan, Y.-Q. & Lu, L.-L. 2011. An information security maturity evaluation mode. *Procedia Engineering*, 24, 335–339.

Gordon, L. A. & Loeb, M. P. 2002. The economics of information security investment. *ACM Transactions on Information and System Security*, 5, 438–457.

Gordon, L. A. & Loeb, M. P. 2006. *Managing cyber-security resources: A cost-benefit analysis*. McGraw-Hill.

Gordon, L. A., Loeb, M. P. & Lucyshyn, W. 2003. Sharing information on computer systems security: An economic analysis. *Journal of Accounting and Public Policy*, 2, 461–485.

Gordon, L. A., Loeb, M. P., Lucyshyn, W. & Zhou, L. 2015. The impact of information sharing on cybersecurity underinvestment: A real options perspective. *Journal of Accounting and Public Policy*, 34, 509–519.

Gordon, L. A., Loeb, M. P. & Zhou, L. 2016. Investing in cybersecurity: Insights from the Gordon-Loeb Model. *Journal of Information Security*, 7, 49–59. Security, 17, 303–307.

Greene, F. 2015. Cybersecurity detective controls—monitoring to identify and respond to threats. *ISACA*, 5.

Grunske, L. & Joyce, D. 2008. Quantitative risk-based security prediction for component-based systems with explicitly modeled attack profiles. *The Journal of Systems and Software*, 81, 1327–1345.

Hausenblas, M. & Nguyen, R. 2019. *Native container image scanning in Amazon ECR*. Amazon Web Services (AWS).

Henriques De Gusmão, A. P., Camara E Silva, L., Maisa, M., Silva, A., Poleto, T. & Costa, A. P. C. S. 2016. Information security risk analysis model using fuzzy decision theory. *International Journal of Information Management*, 26, 25–34.

Huang, C. D. & Behara, R. S. 2013. Economics of information security investment in the case of concurrent heterogeneous attacks with budget constraints. *International Journal of Production Economics*, 141, 255–268.

Huang, C. D., Hu, Q. & Behara, R. S. 2008. An economic analysis of the optimal information security investment in the case of a risk-averse firm. *International Journal of Production Economics*, 114, 793–704.

Humble, J. & Molesky, J. 2011. Why DevOps must adopt continuous delivery to enable continuous delivery? *The Journal of Information Technology Management*, 24(8), 6–12.

Huntsman. 2017. *ASD essential eight: Patching and vulnerability management—how to get it right*. Viewed March–May 2020. www.huntsmansecurity.com.

Information Systems Audit and Control Association (ISACA). 2009. *The risk IT framework*. Viewed April 2020. www.isaca.org.

Information Systems Audit and Control Association (ISACA). 2017. *Vulnerability assessment*. Viewed April 2020. www.isaca.org.

International Standards Organization (ISO). Viewed March–May 2020. www.iso.org

Jegers, M. 1991. Prospect theory and the risk-return relation: Some Belgian evidence. *Academy of Management Journal*, 34, 215–225.

Johnson, A. 2009. Business and security executives' view of information security investment drivers: Results from a Delphi study. *Information Privacy Security*, 5, 3–27.

Joshi, C. & Singh, U. K. 2017. Information security risks management framework: A step towards mitigating security risks in university network. *Journal of Information Security and Applications*, 35, 128–137.

Jouini, M., Rabai, L. B. A. & Khedri, R. 2015. A multidimensional approach towards a quantitative assessment of security threats. *Procedia Computer Science*, 52, 507–514.

Kemkhadze, N. 2004. *Information and optimisation in investment and risk measurement*. PhD, University of Warwick, Warwick Business School.

Kissoon, T. 2019a. *Optimum spending on cybersecurity measures.* Emerald Publishing Ltd., Transforming Government: People, Process and Policy.

Kissoon, T. 2019b. Optimum spending on cybersecurity measures: Part II. *Journal of Information Security.*

Kolkowska, E., Karlsson, F. & Hedström, K. 2017. Towards analysing the rationale of information security non- compliance: Devising a value-based compliance analysis method. *The Journal of Strategic Information Systems*, 26, 39–57.

Kossiakoff, A. & Sweet, W. N. 2003. *Systems engineering principles and practice.* John Wiley and Sons, Inc., pp. 98–106.

Lavine, M. K. 2007. *Cyber security information sharing in the United States: An empirical study including risk management and control implications, 2000–2003.* PhD, City University London.

Lee, S., Kim, S., Choi, K. & Shon, T. 2017. Game theory-based security vulnerability quantification for social internet of things. *Future Generation Computer Systems*, Online, 1–9.

Lee, Y. J., Kauffman, R. J. & Sougstad, R. 2011. Profit maximizing firm investments in customer information security. *Decision Support Systems*, 51, 904–920.

Leuprecht, C., Skillicorn, D. B. & Tait, V. E. 2016. Beyond the castle Model of cyber-risk and cyber-security. *Government Information Quarterly*, 33, 250–257.

Lundberg, K. & Warvsten, A. 2020. *Automated fuzzy logic risk assessment and its role in a DevOps workflow.* Master's thesis, Lund University, Department of Computer Science.

Mayadunne, S. & Park, S. 2016. An economic model to evaluate information security investment of risk-taking small and medium enterprises. *International Journal of Production Economics*, 182, 519–530.

Mortazavi-Alavi, R. 2016. *A risk-driven investment model for analysing human factors in information security.* PhD, University of East London.

Mukhopadhyay, A., Chatterjee, S., Saha, D., Mahanti, A. & Sadhukhan, S. K. 2013. Cyber-risk decision models: To insure IT or not? *Decision Support Systems*, 56, 1–26.

National Cyber Security Centre. 2016. *Summary of risk methods and frameworks.* United Kingdom.

National Institute of Standards and Technology (NIST). Viewed March–May 2020. www.nist.gov.

Nazareth, D. & Choi, J. 2015. A system dynamics model for information security management. *Information Management*, 52, 123–134.

Ochoa, D. C. R., Correia, R., Peña, J. I. & Población, J. 2015. Expropriation risk, investment decisions and economic sectors. *Economic Modelling*, 48, 326–342.

Orojloo, H. & Azgomi, M. A. 2017. A game-theoretic approach to model and quantify the security of cyber-physical systems. *Computers in Industry*, 88, 44–57.

Palmaers, T. 2013. *Implementing a vulnerability management process.* SANS Institute.

Pettigrew, A. 2009. *The politics of organizational decision-making.* Routledge.

Posey, C., Roberts, T. L., Lowry, P. B. & Hightower, R. T. 2014. Bridging the divide: A qualitative comparison of information security thought patterns between information security professionals and ordinary organizational insiders. *Information & Management,* 51, 551–567.

Project Management Institute. Viewed January 19, 2022. www.pmi.org/disciplined-agile/process/introduction-to-dad.

Purser, S. A. 2004. Improving the ROI of the security management process. *Computer Security,* 23, 542–546.

Rahimian, F., Bajaj, A. & Bradley, W. 2016. Estimation of deficiency risk and prioritization of information security controls: A data-centric approach. *International Journal of Accounting Information Systems,* 20, 38–64.

Rhee, H. S., Ryu, Y. U. & Kim, C.-T. 2012. Unrealistic optimism on information security management. *Computer & Security,* 31, 221–232.

Ringland, G. 2002. *Scenarios in business.* John Wiley & Sons.

Rodriguez, E. 2010. *Knowledge management applied to enterprise risk management.* PhD, Aston University.

Rose, S., Spinks, N. & Canhoto, A. I. 205. *Management research: Applying the principles.* Abingdon, Oxon: Routledge.

Rue, R., Pfleeger, S. & Ortiz, D. 2007. A framework for classifying and comparing models of cyber security investment to support policy and decision-making. *The Sixth Workshop on the Economics of information security (WEIS07).*

Ryan, J. J. C. H., Mazzuchi, T. A., Ryan, D. J., Lopez De La Cruz, J. & Cooke, R. 2012. Quantifying information security risks using expert judgment elicitation. *Computers & Operations Research,* 39, 774–784.

Saleh, M. S. & Alfantookh, A. 2015. A new comprehensive framework for enterprise information security risk management. *Procedia Economics and Finance,* 28, 243–248.

Shameli-Sendi, A., Aghababaei-Barzegar, R. & Cheriet, M. 2016. Taxonomy of information security risk assessment (ISRA). *Computer & Security,* 57, 14–30.

Sharkasi, O. 2015. Addressing cybersecurity vulnerabilities. *ISACA,* 5.

Talbot, J. & Jakeman, M. 2008. *SRMBOK: Security risk management body of knowledge.* Carlton South: Risk Management Institution of Australasia Limited.

The Mitre Institute. 2007. *MITRE systems engineering (SE) competency model.* Version 1, pp. 10, 40–41.

Tsiakis, T. & Stephanides, G. 2005. The economic approach of information security. *Computer & Security,* 24, 105–108.

UNIDEVOPS. 2022. *Critical phases of DevOps lifecycle.* DevOps University.

Van Schaik, P., Jeske, D., Onibokun, J., Coventry, L., Jansen, J. & Kusev, P. 2017. Risk perceptions of cyber-security and precautionary behaviour. *Computers in Human Behaviour,* 75.

Van Staalduinen, M. A., Khan, F., Gadag, V. & Reniers, G. 2017. Functional quantitative security risk analysis (QSRA) to assist in protecting critical process infrastructure. *Reliability Engineering & System Safety*, 157, 23–24.

Von Neuman, J. & Morgenster, O. 2007. *Theory of games and economic behaviour*. Princeton, NJ: Princeton University Press.

Von Solms, R. & Van Niekerk, J. 2008. From information security to cyber security. *Computer & Security*, 38, 97–102.

Webb, J., Ahmad, A., Maynard, S. B. & Shanks, G. 2014. A situation awareness model for information security risk management. *Computer & Security*, 57, 14–30.

Wiseman, R. M. & Gormez-Mejia, L. R. 1998. A behavioural agency model of managerial risk taking. *Academy of Management Review*, 23, 133–153.

Wu, Y., Feng, G., Wang, N. & Liang, H. 2015. Game of information security investment: Impact of attack types and network vulnerability. *Expert Systems with Applications*, 42, 6132–6146.

Wynn, J. 2014. *Threat assessment and remediation analysis (TARA)*. Mitre Corporation.

Yevseyeva, I., Morisset, C. & Van Moorsel, A. 2016. Modeling and analysis of influence power for information security decisions. *Performance Evaluation*, 98, 36–51.

Zavgorodniy, V., Lukyanov, P. & Nazarov, S. 2014. The selection algorithm of mechanisms for management of information risks. *Procedia Computer Science*, 31.

Index

Note: Page numbers in *italics* indicate a figure and page numbers in **bold** indicate a table on the corresponding page.

Printed in the United States
by Baker & Taylor Publisher Services